SHORT STORIES

The Story of a Refugee

By

Rea-Silvia Costin, P.E.

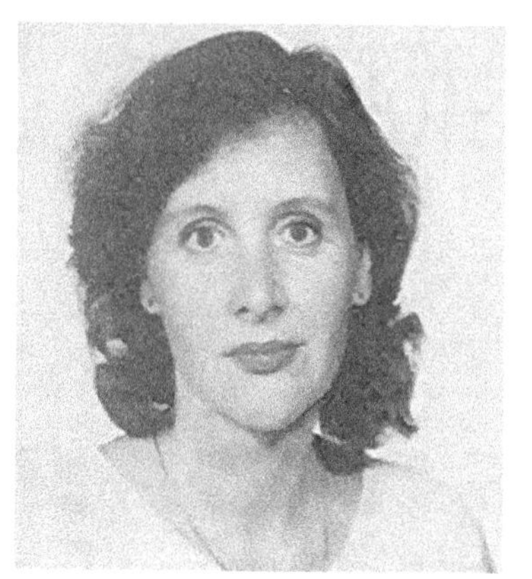

To my Family,

My father- Stefan Costin, mother-Steliana, brother- Radu and sister-Magdalena,

Who are my roots and my strength.

It is said that the character of a child is molded by environmental factors, by family values, by education, by parental guidance. All that is true, as it is also true that some characteristics one is born with and remains unchanged for the duration of one's life.

REA-SILVIA COSTIN, P.E. @ 2016

Table of Contents

... about me

The need to write came into my life unexpectedly and with such force that it left me no choice but to follow.

I published my first book *Short Stories: The Story of a Refugee* –First Edition-with Vantage Press in 1997. In 2003, I published the first book of a trilogy, *Thiana-AVDELA-A Macedonian Village in the Northwestern Greece: Thiana's Native Land* and in 2004; I published the second volume of the trilogy *ATHENS* with iUniverse. American Publishing Company has published the third book of the trilogy, *America-The Final Destination* in 2006.

American Publishing Company also has published my first poetry book: *Pearls on a String: Love Songs* –Volume I- on December 13, 2006, and the second volume in 2010. In 2010 I also published *"Different Tales: A Children's Book"* with American Publishing Company.

My poetry is published in *The Best Poems and Poets of 2001, 2002, 2003, and 2005, The Theatre of the Mind,* and *The Celebrations of Honors* as well as *Who's Who in Poetry 2004, 2005, and 2007* editions by the International Library of Poetry. In May 2002, I obtained my Laureate Certificate from the International Library of Poets. I am the recipient of the Editor's Choice Award, 2002, 2003, 2005, and 2007 from the poetry.com site as well as the President's Award for Excellence in Literature from the National Authors Registry.

In January 2005, I joined the Poets.com Workshop under the pen name of Frantzi500 (my nickname).

I was born in Greece and raised in Romania.

I am a Professional Engineer.

What does poetry mean to me?

It's a way to express deep feelings, to share with others my philosophy and understanding of life, and to give testimony of my faith in God.

Mother

My mother is my role model. My whole life I loved and deeply respected my mother. She is one of those exceptional individuals who totally forget themselves for the good of others, one whose moral standards are above any reproach.

Everything she taught us, everything I watched my mother do over the years, it became my way of life, my way of thinking about people, my way of thinking about what is right and wrong, about how one has to conduct himself or herself in life.

My mother was born in a little mountain village in the Pindu Mountains of northwestern Greece named Avdela. I heard so many stories from my mother about Avdela that I think I was there. My Mother's family had a house built up on the hill in Avdela where the family spent the summers. They also had a house in Grevena, a larger town located at the foot of the mountains.

Avdela was a summer place for the people whose main occupation was shepherding. My mother's father-Iani (my grandfather) had horses and used to do trade with lumber. The family had five children, three boys namely, Tache, Apostol and Vangheli, and two girls namely Maritza and Thiana (short from Steliana)- my mother.

Everything was fine until my grandfather died. There were five children aged five to fifteen left to raised up by my grandmother Caliopi.

And my grandmother Caliopi had raised them, and sent the boys to college by doing whatever she knew how to do: quilting rugs, selling them and renting the big house in Grevena. The girls, especially my mother's older sister, Maritza, helped her mother.

There were so many stories I heard from my mother about their simple yet happy lives over there, how close their family was and how they all helped one another. My mother raised us in the same spirit.

There were stories about her father being spotted by masked highwaymen on their way from Grevena to Avdela on horseback; there were stories about my grandmother baking bread in the family's big oven(more like a enclosed fire pit)in the front yard; about my mother being bitten by a viper on the mountains and how her father saved her life by wrapping her foot within the belly of a just-cut lamb; about my mother being sick with meningitis and everybody expecting her to die and my mother getting better and wearing the new shoes they prepared to bury her with and wearing them to the Church at Eastertime.

When my mother was fourteen years old, she left Avdela and went with a cousin to Romania to study at the Romanian schools. She did it on her own and became a teacher. Then she went back to Greece to stay there and live with her family. Her fate, however, was different. She met and married my father, a Romanian, and spent the better part of her life in Romania.

When I was a child, I remember my mother saying over and over again that her only wish was to go back in Greece to her natal village, Avdela, and just kiss the natal land. At that time the Communist Regime in Romania was very strict. Nobody was traveling outside Romania, and my mother's wish did not became reality for many years.

Finally when she got a chance to go there, everything was changed. The brothers had demolished the old house on the hill and taken the stones to build themselves houses closer in the valley. The brothers' wives took over the houses, and my mother was just a guest in her own natal place.

When I was in Greece, my mother's brothers didn't invite me to visit Avdela. My Mother's older brother, Tache, was the Mayor of the village for a good many years.

Now that we are all in the U.S.A., she still thinks of Avdela and their life as children there. There is where her soul belongs.

Focsani

My father was born in Focsani, a small town in Moldova. Moldova is the northeastern part of Romania, bordering the former Soviet Union. Now days, on the eastern border with Romania, across from the Prut River, is the Republic Of Moldova. This State used to be part of the greater Romania after the First World War (1919); it was called Basarabia and its people speak Romanian. Moldova region east of the Prut River is the part of Romania with the richest traditions and history, the part where people are kind and hospitable, soft-talking and story-telling; the part that has rich, fertile land and is famous for its vineyards, the part where there is a string of old churches called "Monasteries" where the monks and nuns still live to this day.

My grandfather, Nicolai (Jirca), was a big, tall, proud man. He was a prosperous merchant. His trade was in fruits and vegetables, and the family owned a fruit and gems factory located just across the street from the family's house. My grandmother, Lina (short for Magdalena), was a strong, beautiful woman, richly clothed (my sister was named after her and physically resemble her). There were six children in the family, four boys and two girls. One of the boys, Ionel, died young.

The family's house, where my father grew up, was left as dowry to the oldest daughter, Maria. I visited and spent many vacations in that house as a child. It was located on a picturesque cobblestone street called "Two Pecans Street". The house had a wide, covered terrace in front of a row of rooms, all having the entrance doors from the porch. In the summer-time, we ate on the terrace, as I remember. The house was surrounded by beds of flowers. There was an old pecan tree in the back yard.

Maria had bad luck. She was a kind-hearted, very beautiful woman. Now, that I think, all the members of my father's family were strong, beautiful people, both men and women. Maria's father arranged to marry her when she was only sixteen years old to a rich, older man. She was very unhappy. I don't know if she got a divorce, or the older man died, but after that Maria found a man she loved deeply named Costian. This man did not treat Maria as well as she deserved. Many times as a child going to sleep in the room adjacent to their bedroom, I heard them arguing late in the night. That's what happened when Maria had a stroke later on and remained paralyzed for sixteen years in the care of her younger sister, Olga. She was arguing with Costian.

Costian had a good job at the post office. I remembered the time when we were having breakfast on the terrace and my brother Radu, a small child at the time, started making fun of Costian's nose. Both Radu and I could not stop laughing. We were thinking that his nose looked rather like a pickle jar. Costian got very angry and followed my brother with his cane raised in his hand. But my brother escaped by climbing on the roof of the outside restroom. After that Maria did not invite us to spend the summer vacations in her house any longer.

Fragrant, white and yellow wild flowers surrounded the house, and I remember taking a bath in a small tub put outside in the garden among the wild flowers. The flowers were so tall that nobody could see me.

I remember eating green peas with fresh cut dill, a favorite meal cooked by Maria, at lunchtime, on the terrace. Even now, when I smell fresh cut dill, I remember Maria and her house in Focsani. I remember the impeccable set breakfast table, with its white, starched linens, with silver goblets especially for eggs. I remember Maria teaching me how to boil eggs to perfection: count to 200 after the water starts boiling, and then put them in cold water. I remember all this because Mother did not have time for setting breakfast tables, or the luxury of long talks. She was working.

I remember one morning when Olga came by to take Maria to the open market. It was very early in the morning, about 5:00 A.M. I was in bed pretending to be asleep and looking at Maria as she prepared to go out. When Olga first came, I thought she looked very beautiful in her elegant cloths, but by the time Maria finished dressing up and putting her makeup on, she was even more beautiful. After they left, my sister Mady and my cousin Adriana, Olga's daughter, and I started to rummaged though the closets. Ewe especially liked to look through Costians' closets. We were hoping to find small treasures, like a lost earing, or ribbons, or small pices of cloth to make dresses for our dolls. When Maria and Olga returned and found what we were doing they scolded us severely.

Maria's youngest sister, Olga, was more realistic then her sister. She loved to read novels and love stories, but built her life on solid ground. She started out by working as a telephone operator at the Telephone Company. She liked to dress up, and as I remember she liked to wear those fancy hats.

Olga married a man who took care of her and provided for her. Their house was well kept, and her pantry was always stocked with food, even when times were hard and you could not find any food on the market. She always had plenty of the best foods. I remember the smoked hams and sausages, the fresh meats and poultry, especially because we, in Bucharest, didn't have any. Olga's husband worked for a company that produced wines. They always had the best wine. Both of my father's sisters knew how to cook very well. My father also knew how to cook. He claimed he learned by watching and helping his mother in the kitchen. The Moldavian people did not cook just for one person. They did not know how. They cooked plenty, to feed an entire army, the best foods the best pastries. Every autumn my father used to make big jars (10 kilograms) of different fruit gems, golden jars with orange preserves, white cherries, and wild black cherries, and put cabbage in a big barrel to sour for the winter use, and he canned pickles and green bell peppers stuffed with shredded carrots mixed with shredded red cabbage preserved in vinegar. He knew how to prepare fresh sausages and all king of culinary specialties.

Focsani is the kind of small provincial town called "the town of old maids" because nothing ever happens there. People are content to live an easy, comfortable life, with plenty of good food and even better wine. My father had cousins and relatives in Focsani. Everybody knew everybody else. They went for afternoon visits and coffee and everybody knew everybody else's stories. The town has a main street "Corso" where the people went in the afternoons for walks, where the town's movie theater was, where the restaurants were located. There was a public Garden where the people went for long walks. The main transportation was walking and riding the carriages drawn by horses, as a special treat. Everything was within the walking distance.

Lost

BUCHAREST, ROMANIA, 1950's

I remember the house I grew up in back in Romania. It was an old house, maybe a hundred years old, built in the original Byzantine style, with great, thick brick walls, plastered inside and outside (the façade), with a full basement and beautiful venetian stuccos trimming the high ceilings and doors. The house did not have all the comforts of a modern house, but had the beauty and elegance of a small palace. The house was located within walking distance from Calea Victoriei, the "Corso" of Bucharest, and within walking distance of the most beautiful park Cismigiu. Cismigiu consisted of the former gardens of the palace with the same name. The Government took over the palace, but the gardens were transformed into a public park.

Now, from my house, if you looked out of the window of one of the front rooms, you could see Cismigiu Palace with its gardens at the end of the street leading straight from my house.

I remember being a little girl, maybe three years old-really my first conscious memory. My mother had just brought in the clean laundry freshly smelling of the outside spring air. I remember sitting on top of the bed, my mother dressing me up in a fresh, ruffled, red-and-white checkered dress. I remember asking my mother to fix my favorite hairdo, which was big curl pinned up on top of my head and set with a big red checkered ribbon. I was getting ready to go outside and play with other children.

I was filled with joy and trepidation waiting to get out. I told my mother I was to play with children in a nearby playing ground, but in my mind I knew differently. I had already made up my mind to go to Cismigiu Gardens, where I heard the bigger children went. I had a vague idea that the park was just straight ahead from my house and I was confident I could make it on my own without telling anybody. The truth be told, I knew deep inside, that if I was to tell my mother, she was not going to let me go. I was filled with an adventurous feeling and ready to go in the exploration of new grounds.

So, I left the house sometime during mid-morning and went straight ahead on the street leading from our house to Cismigiu. I passed the nearby playground called Gradinita (little garden) where the other children were playing and went farther until the street ended. There it was another street, wider, that was perpendicular on the street leading from my house. Now, just across this street were the Cismigiu Gardens, but that I did not know at that time.

Now, here I stopped and looked around me. I did not recognize anything anymore. Worse, I turned around and now I got totally disoriented. I forgot which direction I came from and I could not go back home. Everything looked different, the streets so big and wide, cars crossing the road and me, a small girl, totally lost.

I remember getting near a power pole and starting to cry. Nobody was nearby. Finally, a man passed by and asked me why I cried. I didn't remember exactly what he asked me and how it came that I went with him to his house.

I remembered during that day playing with children in and out of some cars parked on a big empty terrain. I remember having a good time and having totally forgotten about my parents. When the evening came and the people took me inside their home, I remember that I started to cry again and ask about my parents. It was the man's name day, Saint Gheorge, and they were celebrating with food and wine. I remember their offering me sweets, but now I wanted my mother and I refused to eat anything. Finally, I remember my mother and father appearing in the doorway of the people's house and looking at me; my father wearing his overcoat and his hat, his heavy briefcase in one hand and the other around my mother's shoulders'; my mother with a scarf covering her hair and clutching in her arms my little brother-Radu. (That's how I know I was three years old at the time, as Radu is two years younger than me and he was a small baby at the time).

Probably, as small as I was, I knew where I lived, or remembered the home telephone number, or the people who found me reported to the Police.

Meanwhile at home, as I learned later, Mother was going totally out of her mind with worry and trying to find me through the Police. My older sister, Mady, who was in charge of me, took all the blame for not watching over me.

My House

The house we owned in Romania, the house I grew up in, the house that sometime I dream of, was an old house that my parents brought when they came back from Greece, in 1947.

The World War II had divided Europe in two: the free countries to the West, and the countries behind the Iron Curtain to the East. Romania was one of them. Greece belonged to the free World. My Father, who was A Romanian Citizen, working in Greece, as the Director of Romanian Schools in Salonika, Greece, was forced to come back to Romania. My mother who is Greek, worked as a teacher at the same school. There she met and married my father. I, of all the children was born in Salonika, Greece.

When my parent brought the house, it was a charming house, with wild roses climbing the thick walls, with Italian stuccos adorning the inside and outside of the house. The house had the main quarters up front, a total eight great rooms with tall windows full of sun, with high ceilings and gleaming hard wood floors. In the back, it had the servants' quarters consisting of two rows of smaller buildings, set to the side of the main house toward the back yard. The main house had two entrances; the front entrance, which we used, leading to a beautiful hallway from which there were, to the right two front rooms facing the street, and the left a third room Also to the left was the entrance to the utility hallway, to the attic and basement.

The secondary entrance leads to a long back hallway leading to the last four rooms. Of course, originally the house was built to serve one family and its servants. The Communist Regine forced a lot of people upon us to live in the house. There were people who never owned anything in their entire life, and did not have a place to live, people who came in the Country's Capital from villages. The Government decreed that every person has the right to inhabit so many square meters of living space. The fact that we owned the house did not matter. We were not asked. We were considered lucky that we were allowed to live there. In the beginning, I remember, we were forced into the front two rooms, facing the street, only. There were six of us: my parents, and us the three children, and a young girl named Vica, who lived with us and took care of us.

Then, of course each room of the house was housing a family. They all used the back entrance and the back hallway as their kitchen. There were two restrooms for the entire house, located at the end of the back hallway, next to the back entrance. The two rows of servants' buildings were now occupied by other two families. Joyous events and tragedies happened it that house; children were born and people died in that house.

I remember the Rezman family, who lived in one of the servants' buildings; the man was of German heritage from Timisoara, his wife Margareta, and their two little girls, about my age, Louisa and Simona. Many a time I played with Louisa in the back yard, with our dolls. Then there were Irma and Vasili Grigorutza. Irma was of Hungarian Origin. They had a little boy called Vasilica. Then there was Valerica, again of Hungarian origin who was married with Carol Viallard, of French origin, and there was Sandulescu and his wife who worked in the neighborhood shoe repair shop.

I remember the time when Grigorutza had an affair with Margareta, and they were caught by Irma. I remember that afterwards Margareta willed herself to die. I remember the Rezman family and my friend Louisa moving back to Timisoara.

I remember Valerica trying to kill herself. I remember the Sandulescu family, both of them dying and other families moving in. I remember the Vlad family who wants to take the back house from us and sued us. I remember Gica, who was a drunkard, and sang all night long when the three of us had to study for the college exams.

I remember Engineer Vasili Rosu. Irma was taking care of him at the time. I remember when Irma hit the old man and broke his shoulder. Then, Engineer Vasili Rosu called my parents and asked them to build a wall to physically separate his room from Irma's. And I remember my mother taking pity on him and doing so. Since then Engineer Vasili Rosu, a countrywide renowned Hydrotechnical Engineer, was part of our family. We would go summers in vacations and take him with us. We inherited "his golden bracelet", his job trade, his profession, the three of us.

As time passed, and we grew older, the many families living in the house started to move out, to better living quarters. Gradually, the house became ours again.

Then, we started to remodel it. We were all students at the time. We took Vasili, a fine plasterer, in to stay with us for a whole year. And Vasili with our help restored the house to its original grandeur. We scraped away the many layers of paint and revealed the original gold painting of the interior stucco. Vasili plastered the walls for the entire house anew, and we choose different colors for each room to match the color of the antiques ceramic stoves. The house was again a grand house, with bedrooms, dining room, and kitchen as was originally designed. We installed a central heat system and remodeled the bathroom.

When we finished with everything, I left the country, and then my entire family left after me.

I still love that house, and often dream of it, as it is my house, and it is part of me.

After the fall of the communist regime in Eastern Europe in 1989, and the "iron curtain" parted, I succeed to go back to Romania for a short visit (in my two-week vacation).

I applied for, and the new democratic regime restituted our house back to us. We did some repairs to the house; installed a new roof, restored the façade, and put a new fence, all done in our short vacation time. We think to put is for sale, as we are established now in the USA, and nobody could live over in two continents- at least not us.

Christmas

BUCHAREST, ROMANIA 1950'S

The first Christmas, I remember was when I was four or five years old. I say, I think I was four or five years old, as my brother, Radu, who is two years younger than me, was around.

I remember the night before the St. Nicholas Day, which is December 6. The custom, at least at our house was, that St. Nicholas brought candies. We, the children, got new stockings, the cotton ones, which looked like macaroni on our legs, tight high, brown, or gray to keep us warm during the heavy winter months, stuffed with candies. I remember my brother and I talking the night before the St. Nicholas Day.

As I grew up, I was closer to my brother, Radu, than my sister. My sister was already at school, or had friends of her own, but I remember my brother and I going outside on winter days to play with other children at a place nearby called Gradinitza, which means little garden. My brother was constantly clinging on me, holding my hand, and I felt embarrassed, as I would have liked to look more grown up and more independent to the other children and there I was with my little brother constantly holding on to my arm. I would slap his little hand away, and he, trustingly, would put it right back on my arm. Our feet would get frozen in the hard freeze outside, but the two of us would stay outside and play with the other children.

For maybe the first two years of his life, my brother looked like a girl, because my mother would dress him in our dresses, which my sister and I had outgrown. There was not enough money, or time, to buy him boy's clothes. He had beautiful hair (and he has it to this day), blonde, long and curly. He was chubby and dressed in girls' cloths.

The night I remember, before St. Nicholas Day, my brother was telling me that he was planning not to sleep all night, but wait until St. Nicholas came. Then, he would pull at his long underwear strings and St. Nicholas would fall down and then we would know for sure if it was St. Nicholas, or my father. It was dark and warm in the house. We were tacked away in our little beds, and could see the light coming from the fire in the stove. At that time we, the children were sleeping in the little room and my parents slept in the big room next door. The little room was always warm and cozy. The big room was cold. Probably at that time, we had the use of the entrance hallway and the two rooms up front, and nothing else of the house. The little room had a blue ceramic stove and in the beginning there was enough fire wood to warm up the rooms. I remember often staying on the floor in front of the open grate of the stove and toasting slices of white bread and then putting butter on them. Other times we grilled stakes on the open fire inside the stove in the same room. Other time, we ate a roasted turkey, each of us nibbling from the same tray in that same room. It seems as if we grew up in this room. I do not remember if we had a girl taking care of us children at that time.

I remember for sure having one when I was six years old. She was Vica, a young country girl, who was always cleaning the house, doing the laundry, taking care of us, the children, and doing my mother's hair.

That year, I remember we had the Christmas tree in the big room up front. The tree was as tall as the room, 12 to 15 feet tall. We had real candles to light up the tree and fireworks at small scale, called "artificii" which we lighted on the night before Christmas. We had, each of us, our favorite Christmas ornaments. Mine was a glass clown face painted in vivid colors, my sister's was a lamp and my brother's a house.

I remember lying in bed next to my mother and "working" on her. I was telling my mother that my wish for Christmas was for Santa Claus, whom we called "Mos Craciun" to bring me a doll's carriage. I told her over and over again. I remember precisely that in the back of my mind I knew I was working on my mother, because I knew she was the one who brought the presents, but I pretended to think that Mos Craciun was bringing them.

At that Christmas all of us got their wishes. I got the doll's carriage, my sister got a doll's bed, and my brother got a wooden train. We were in the big room, at the toe of the Christmas tree and I was so happy I was spinning around with the carriage. I remember being quite cold in that room.

I do not remember every Christmas, besides this one, but I know every year we had a big Christmas tree put up in the front room. We and father went and brought a tree each year from the open market and put it up in the front room and decorated it.

We kept the Christmas tree tradition for all our life.

The Doll

BUCHAREST, ROMANIA 1950'S

Ever since I remember, I loved dolls.

I remember playing dolls and house with my friend Louisa in the back yard of our house in Bucharest. My friend Louisa and her family rented a small building toward the back of our house. Not the father one; that one was rented by the Madame Sandulescu and her husband and they always acted as if the back yard belonged in exclusivity to them. There was a lilac bush in the back yard, which bloomed beautiful in spring time, and a vine spread over a wooden frame, like a roof, making a perfect place to have lunch or dinner evenings. And the Sandulescu family enjoyed the back yard and often had grilled fish over an open fire and ate beneath the vine, evenings and Sundays at lunchtime.

Every time, we, the children went in the back yard to play it was as if we were intruding. And it was our property, after all. But during the weekdays, when Sandulescu was working in the neighborhood shoe repair shop and his wife was helping him, my friend Louisa and I, and sometimes her sister Simona played "house". I would drag an old suitcase from the house and arrange the interior of it like a regular house.

We had doll furniture and doll stove and doll pans, and we were making dresses for our dolls, playing house, cleaning up the house, and cooking for the dolls, as regular mothers would do for their children. I would carry my doll around in the carriage and Louisa would do the same. I do not remember my sister ever participating. I was mainly me and Louisa.

Later Louisa's mother, Margareta, died unexpectedly, and her family moved back to Timisoara, where her father's family came from. I *lost my friend and never payed house again.*

I remember seeing a doll in Tincutza's house, in Ploiesti, which I had my heart set on. This doll was the first doll I have seen that closed her eyes and could say "Mama". She was the size of a small child, all dressed up in a long purple gown with beige laces. We, children were not allowed to play with it, just look at it.

One summer we were coming back from a summer vacation with our parents. I do not remember exactly how old I was at the time. I remember that for some reason, my parents promised me that when we got back from vacation, we would stop first in Ploiesti, to see my Uncle Gorg, and they would give me Tincutza's doll.

We were traveling by train, and when we arrived at the train station and I recognized the train station as Bucharest and not Ploiesti, I refused to go on the Tram ("Tramway") and go home. I remained on the train platform, crouched down, and started crying and yelling. A big crowd formed immediately around me, and my parents could do nothing. I was very frustrated about the doll, but more upset because my parents would lie to and deceive me. Usually, I was a quit child, who liked more to observe that to act, and in any other circumstances, I would have been mortified by such behavior. But at the time I was enraged beyond comprehension.

I never got Tincutza's doll, but when I was about fourteen years old, In Bucharest, there was the first pot-war German Exhibit and my father promised me he would buy me a doll that closed her eyes. He probably remembered my heart break over Tincutza's doll. I was a big girl, going to high Scholl now, but I remember being so excited about the prospect of father buying me a doll, that I talked myself into not being so excited. I thought if I wished for something so much, I might not get it. Something would go wrong, and I would not get the doll. But father kept his promise and took me to the German Exhibit and bought me a doll with curly blond hair and blue eyes that closed as I moved the doll. I cherished that doll, and made cloths for her and set her up on my bed and looked at her. Later, when I left Romania, my mother sent me the doll. I took it with me in the airplane from Greece to the USA. I thought if I keep it outside in my handbag, would not be damaged. On the contrary. Keeping it there unprotected, the doll was damaged going through customs and changing the airplanes at the Kennedy Airport in New-York to Jacksonville.

I still have a doll from Romania. It is a "tarancutza", a country dressed doll in traditional Romanian country clothing, which I have had since childhood, and it's now on a self in my bedroom, in Jacksonville.

As I heard later from her sister, Louisa married when she was seventeen years old and got her children to take care of. I, on the other hand, did not get married, and did not have any children.

Calarasi

BARAGAN, ROMANIA, LATE 1950'S

My father's youngest brother, Costica, was a very tall (over two meters tall), handsome, distinguished looking man, with a military bearing. He used to be a navy commander on his own ship, before the WWII and earned his medals and distinctions in battles.

After the was and after the Communist Regime took hold in Romania, he was forced to leave his house in Turnu Severin, on the Danube River, and was forced to move to Baragan, overnight.

Now, Baragan was in Romania what Siberia was in Russia; a place of hardship, a place in the middle of swamps and open fields, isolated from the civilized world.

Costica was married at that time with Ileana, and they had a small girl about my age, Roxana. Ileana came from an aristocratic family (her maiden name was Coanda) and had inherited a small palace in Turnu Severin. Ileana was my uncle's second wife. His first wife was from Focsani, a young, beautiful French woman, whom Costica loved very much. But the young wife could not live with a Navy husband, and during her husband prolonged absence, she run away with a local pharmacist, as I heard the story. Then, Costica married Ileana, who was maybe a few years older and not so pretty, but she had all the education, manners and rigorous upbringing of her social class. Ileana had never had to work on her life. Her parents always had plenty of servants to do everything for her.

Costica, Ileana and their daughter, Roxana, had to move overnight from their house in Turnu Severin with very few of their belongings.

My uncle used to say, afterwards, that if he had known where "they" would take them, then taking a shovel and an axel from their home would have been a wiser choice than some of the silver. ("They" being the Communist Regime and their Secret Service called "Securitate").

On a summer vacation during the late 1950's, I remember, I was invited to visit them in Baragan. Father put me into the train in Bucharest, along with our yellow bicycle, and my uncle waited for me at the train station in Calarasi. Looking back, I think I was the only one from the extended family to visit them in Baragan. When I got there, they made a house for themselves. It was not a great house, but one you could live in. I don't remember precisely, but I think it was made of "kirpici", clay straw walls and a grass roof for there was no forest in Baragan, and no wood supply. It has two rooms with dirt floors. My uncle built it with his own hands. First, I understand, they had to dig what was called a "bordey" into the ground, to have shelter, and then they built the above ground house. There were no other houses nearby, or other people, that I recall. Of course, I was a child at the time, but I don't remember being impressed with it as being a place of total desolation. On the contrary, to me it was a rustic and picturesque place; the open fields were beautiful and the house itself was joyous, and they had the best bacon I ever ate. Ileana, who never had to do anything in her life, adjusted perfectly, or at least I never heard her complaining of anything. She loved my uncle and did whatever she could to help. She learned how to cook and do the laundry, and probably a lot more than I could imagine. She took care of all of them. Between the two of them, she was the backbone of their marriage, the unsinkable one. Their daughter, Roxana, my cousin, was studying home with her mother, and she spoke French much better than me who was studying in school in Bucharest.

Later, they were allowed to move out of Baragan, and they moved to Braila, on the Danube River again. I visited them again, on another summer vacation, when they were in Braila in a rented house. I remember going fishing with them on the Danube River. Both Ileana and Roxana loved ti fish and loved the water.

My uncle found employment as an engineer, and the family later on brought a flat in Galati. After the Communist Regime fall in Romania, in 1989, my cousin, Roxana, tried and succeeded to get her family possessions back. She succeeded to get back the house in Turnu Severin. The irony is that now days the Bucharest largest airport is named "Henry Coanda", a famous air industry pioneer, and close relative of Ileana.

PLOIESTI, ROMANIA, EARLY 1960's

My father's older brother, Gorg, lived in Ploiesti. Ploiesti is a town of medium size located about 60 kilometers north of Bucharest at the foot of the hills and it is well known for its oil and petrol refineries.

Gorg was a big, very kind man with big hands, who wore a mustache. Gorg was the eldest of the six children in my father's family and he helped his father in the vegetable trade. Gorg was never sent to higher schools. He was needed home to help with the work, so the younger brothers could be sent to schools. I remember as a child when Gorg was visiting with us. We used to climb with our feet on his palm and he would lift us effortlessly. He used to wear a laborer's hat called "sapca", which he swore he would cut off with an axel when the Communists were gone.

Gorg had a little house located on the outskirts of Ploiesti, past the railroad tracks. Even with all the new construction going on and the new buildings built, his house never got demolished. Since I first knew him, Gorg lived in the same house. The house was more like the houses one could find in the villages, rather than a town house. It was very picturesque. The house had a row of rooms fronting a big open porch. In the back yard, there were fruit trees, a vegetable garden, the chicken pens, and a pen for the pork. At the front of the house adjoining the street, they built a kiosk, and they sold cigarettes and different small items. That was their work and their way of making a living.

Gorg was a free spirit who never believed that he ought to hold a regular eight-to-five job. That was demeaning to him, as well as working for somebody else, including the Government. That all was beneath his dignity! After all, his father Jirca, my grandfather, whom Gorg resembled the best, was an entrepreneur who never worked for anyone but himself.

Gorg and his second wife, the one that I got to know, and their daughter, Antoaneta, will always hold a special place in my heart.

They were so hospitable, their home was so welcome, and they always had plenty of food. I remember that we used to visit Gorg especially at Eastertime. Then all his trees were blooming, and the vegetable garden was green and fresh. Marieta, his wife, would set the table outside, beneath the pecan tree. They had fresh, green salad, just cut from the garden and smoked pork meat, beacon, and sausages, that they made themselves and kept it in the basement of the house for the entire year. Marieta used to bake special breads for the Easter called "cozonac" and "pasca"(egg bread filled with raisins and cottage cheese). I remember most the warm feeling, the welcome and happiness that filled the little house. Now, we were five in our family, and quite a problem to house and feed. But Marieta and Gorg were never concerned about such trivial matters. They were happy to have us visit. (It seems even then that food was a big issue, because in Bucharest it was scarce, and by the time I left Romania in 1980, you almost could not find anything on the market.)

Gorg was married for the first time with a beautiful woman named Jane, whom he loved very much. Jane died young. I heard stories about Gorg staying put during the bombardment of Ploiesti, during World War II, just to be able to get some parachute silk for Jane to make a blouse. Jane's portrait was hanging on the wall even after Gorg married Marieta.

After Jane's death, Gorg was heartbroken and my mother thought that he would never marry again. He was around sixty years old then. But Gorg surprised everybody and married a young woman and fathered a child. Antoaneta, his daughter was the apple of his eye. But Gorg also loved us children as well.

Marieta came from a big family, and they were very close and always helped each other. Marieta's family even helped us a lot. Marieta had a sister, Tincutza, who was married to a good man with three children from a previous marriage. I remember my parents going to visit Tincutza and her husband Radulescu and staying for long, leisure lunches and dinners, while we were playing with her three children.

Antoaneta took after her father. She never believed in employment and a scheduled life. Antoaneta is now married and has children of her own, and still lives in the same old house located in the neighborhood of Ploiesti called "Gageni".

Tutu (Tzutzu)

ROMANIA 1960'S

Of all my father's relatives , we loved tutu the best.

Tutu and her sister Dui were Mita's (Mitza) daughters. Mita and amy father were first cousins. Mita, at the time I knew her, was a widow, the mother of two daughters and a son called Cornelius. Mita and her family were from the same hometown as my father's family, Focsani. Tutu and Dui were raised to be the perfect wives, nothing more. They finished high school, knew how to cook and how to embroider, how to dress and how to behave properly in society, and basically were waiting to get married.

During the time I remember. Tutu was a young beautiful woman married to Rica. The story, as I heard it from Rica, was that he went on a "proxenia" or matchmaker, to find himself a second wife. His first wife had run away. As he was visiting Mita and her daughters, he first saw Dui, the older one, and liked her. He thought they would get along pretty well, as Dui was also previously married and had two small children. Rica had a son, from his previous marriage, who was not living with him at the time. But then Tutu came into the room, and he was taken with her. He used to tell us, that seeing her at the train station when he left that day, literally took his breath away and stole his heart. Tutu was tall and slender, elegant, with beautiful chestnut hair, and light green eyes, set wide apart and an upturned nose.

I think the first impression when one saw her was of elegance and natural grace, the way she held herself tall and straight, the kind of elegance that no cloths can give.

Rica and Tutu lived in one–room apartment, in a larger building, which was rented to different people. I remember the room being tastefully arranged.

Rica was a man full of life and energy. When everybody was struggling for money, to find food, and to survive, Rica always had money and lived a life of luxury and parties. He was the kind of man, who in any conditions knew how to make money and enjoyed spending it, not only on himself but anyone who happened to be in his company.

I remember a summer vacation we were spending with our parents in Constanta, at the Black Sea beaches. In the evenings our parents took us, the children, on a stroll along shore, "the promenade", where the old Cazina was located. Quite Beatiful! The best my father could do was to treat us to some hard sugar candies, every evening.

One evening we met Tutu and Rica and they took us to the Cazino and treated us, the children, with "cassata" ice cream, an unheard-of luxury for us.

Rica would buy Tutu the most beautiful and extravagant cloths and shoes and take her to the most exclusive restaurants and parties, at a time when ordinary people in Romania were hardly making a living. I remember going to their place for Rica's name day Saint Demetrius and staying late at night and eating all these delicacies that Rica brought and Tutu prepared. When I say we went, the five of us went, and we were always welcomed.

Rica loved Tutu as much as any man could love a woman. At least that was my impression, and I was a young girl by then, about twelve, or thirteen years old. That was my mother's and father's impression too. Tutu was good-hearted and she lent my sister and me, her gorgeous dresses on special occasions, as we grew up. I remember Tutu and Rica taking us, again the five of us, to a baptism of some of their friends, in Pitesti. We were there for three days and partied all the time, danced, ate and slept at their friends' house. Tutu lent me and my sister her dresses, and we had a great time. I remember I was thirteen years old at the time and Tutu dressed me in one of her charcoal-gray taffeta long skirts with a white blouse with bouffant sleeves and red belt. I looked quite grown up and was asked to dance a lot.

Meanwhile Tutu got pregnant and had a little girl, named Roxana, to whom I was the godmother. They baptized Roxana at our home, since we had a big house. The priest came to house with the baptism vase, and baptized the child in a beautiful ceremony with her parent and relatives in attendance. I was twelve years old at the time, and re-member having a hard time holding the baby and reading the Scrip-tures in the same time.

I remember the parties we were having at our house, when Rica was bringing "Caviar" and mourn to eat.

To us Tutu was like Fairy Princess and Rica was her Prince Charm-ing, who swept her off her feet and took good care of her.

Was it trouble in "Paradise" and nobody noticed it? I doubt.

Mita, though, did not like Rica. She wanted her daughter to lavish all her time and attention on her instead of having a life for herself. She continually criticized Rica. I remember Mita visiting us every Sunday afternoon and talking for hours about the same subject-Rica.

Finally Mita got her wish.

She convinced Tutu that the only way to be happy was o divorce Rica. It was an ugly divorce. Tutu asked my mother to witness against Rica, and mother refused.

We all loved Tutu and thought that the divorce was a big mistake. However, Tutu got upset with mother for not taking her part against Rica, and from then on we saw less of her and her daughter. It was as if the lights went out from both Rica's and Tutu's life.

Rica was the one who provided for the house. Besides embroidery, Tutu did not know how to do much of anything. It all sounds crazy, and to this day, I do not understand why she did it, but Tutu divorced Rica and raised the child by herself. She worked all the rest of her life like a dog, doing crafts at home. Her mother, Mita, died of cancer, and recently I heard that Tutu died too. A young Woman. I cannot forgive her mother for what she did to her daughter.

At the divorce, in front of the judge, and everybody in attendance, Rica said that he loved Tutu so much that he would carry her in his arms for few good kilometers to the Cismigiu Gardens. It did not help. Mita was all the more determined to get her daughter back.

What is with people who are so jealous of somebody else's happiness that they try to destroy it at any cost? Or, maybe, it is the Devil himself wiggling its tail and meddling into people's life.

Fagaras

CARPATHIAN MOUNTAINS, ROMANIA, 1960'S

Both of my parents were teaches. They were working all the time, as I remember from growing up, but they had three months paid vacation in the summer, which I also remember wary well. Those were the times when we closed the house in Bucharest, packed our backpacks, and went for three months to see the country. And that meant taking the train to the nearest town and from there hiking in the mountains.

The Carpathian Mountains are beautiful and by and large well-traveled. The highest pick is Fagaras, about 2,500 feet above the sea level. At that time it was less well traveled.

We were making plans well in advance of taking the vacations as the where exactly to go and what to see, using maps and tourist guide books.

This particular year we decided- better said, my brother decided-to climb the Fagaras from one end to the other for the entire length of the crest. We got maps and guide books and mapped out our trip before time to go. My mother, who always was telling us about her upbringing in the Pindu Mountains of Greece, was very sure that we were doing the right thing and we were about to have a great time.

We took the train from Bucharest to the village closest to Fagaras. We spent the first night in a canton located near to the foot of the mountain. There were nice people managing the cabins there, there was food prepared for the tourists and also beds. The beds in those mountain cabins were all in a big great room, one next to the other and one in top of the other. It made no difference who slept where, as far as men and women were concerned. This kind of sleeping arrangements in those mountain cabins was called "prich".

We slept the night there and ate breakfast in the morning. About 8:00 A.M. we started to climb the mountain. The cabin's owner had a shepherd dog, which my brother fed and played with all evening and again in the morning. According to the guide books, the next cabin was eight to ten hours away and we were confident that we could make it before dusk. We had had plenty of other mountain climbing experience to be confident about. On top of it, my mother was always bragging about coming from the mountains and being able to start a fire if we needed one and probably sleeping in the open if we had to. After all it was summer time.

As we started to climb the mountain, we noticed that the shepherd dog followed us. First we thought that he was playing with my brother and that soon he was going to return to his home. After a while, when the dog was still following us, we tried to send him home, but the dog would not go back. He just took after us for good, and nothing would make him turn around and leave us.

The climbing stated to become more difficult. In the beginning, at the foot of the mountain, there were trees, first trees with leaves, then pine trees and then junipers as we went higher and then when we reached the plateau, above 2,000 meters above the sea level, there were no more trees. The mountain was totally bare of any vegetation besides grass. That was something we did not know. Never before in our trips had we encountered bare mountaintops. Always there were trees around, plenty of firewood, and enough shelter.

At a certain moment in the day, it started raining. Mountain rai is really cold. We were not prepared for the rain and cold weather. Our cloths became wet immediately. My sister forgot her glasses at the last stopping point and started to cry that she needed to go back and find her glasses. So, we went back. Now, it started to get dark and foggy and we did not know any longer if we were going forward to the next cabin, or we were going backwards; we lost our sense of direction. The hiking trails were marked by signs, but on the top of the mountain, where people seldom go, the sigs were missing. My brother started crying. And the Rain was coming down on us, cold and sustained. The dog, who refused to go back to his owner and was following us, started to go from one sign to the next, to show us the route. Then when the night was closing on us, and there was nothing else we could do but wait on the bare mountain top to freeze to death, the dog, -we called him Pustiul, or little one, aka Junior- started barking and howling. The shepherds' dogs, way down on the mountain, heard him and answered him, and the shepherds climbed the mountain, came and picked us up, and took us to their place.

Their refuge was set way down the mountain slope and they had a fire going and food prepared- hot corn meal called "mamaliga" with sheep's cheese and milk. They gave us their coats made of sheepskin and put us to sleep in their tent and they spent the night outside.

The next day the shepherds told us that for sure if we were to spend the night outside on the mountaintop, we would have frozen to death, that a lot of other people, city people like us, who think they know the mountain, die there every year.

Of cause our salvation was Pustiul, the shepherd dog.

The second day we cut short our vacation and went back home, to Bucharest. We took Pustiul with us, hiding him in the train beneath the benches, as it was not allowed to travel with dogs in the train.

Pustiul did not like the city atmosphere very much, even though we had a big yard and we were trying to feed him his favored food. The neighbors got to him. He was barking at the wrong times.

* * *

At times, we hear stories about our "Guardian Angels" and we choose to believe them, or not. I do believe that Pustiul- the shepherd dog who trailed after my brother contrary to our efforts to send him back to the cabin, and who saved our lives, it was a "Guardian Angel". He sensed way before us that if we were to remain on the mountain top that night we were to die and he started howling. Have you ever heard a dog howling when his Master was dying?

ROMANIA, 1960's

Both my parents were teachers, or as the called them in Romania, "Professors", because they were teaching high school students. Those who taught elementary school students were called teachers.

The drawbacks of the profession, same as here, were the long hours, the exhausting work with the students, and the small salaries. But among the benefits, especially as we, the children, saw it, was that both my parents got three months of paid vacation in the summertime, from June 1 to September 1.

We made the best of those times. We visited the entire county by train, by car, or on foot. We spent months on the beach at Black Sea, renting a room for the summer from people who lived in Constantza, hiking the Carpathian Mountains and its highest picks carrying our backpacks, visiting beautiful vacation places like "Cheile Bicazului", Busteni, Azuga where the best beer was produced, Predeal, Vatra Dorney; and visiting the historic places and castles, the old monasteries in Moldova.

Every year was something new.

One summer I remember not because it was a great vacation, but because of my grandmother, Caliopi, that we called "Maia" meaning grandmother.

My mother's mother, Caliopi, was born, married and raised her children alone after the death of her husband in Greece, in a little mountain village called Avdela.

Later on, on the children grew up and moved away, she was left to live with her youngest son Vangheli, in Athens. That was the tradition in Greece that the mother stays with her youngest son.

Everything was fine until Vangheli married, and then his wife did not want my grandmother around. Then, they remembered that she had a daughter that lived in Romania, and thought about sending my grandmother to live with us.

My father did not object. There was space enough in our house for one more person, and according to my father, almost everyone was welcomed.

First, they sent my grandmother over in the late 1950's and she stayed for a while. Maya was not happy in Romania. She did not know the places and the people, the language and the customs. My mother was busy with her work and the house, We all were busy with schools and were studying all the time. Nobody had time for her. Not that my grandmother was very demanding. Not at all. She had worked very hard all her life to raise five children by herself. She was a very strong woman and a very intelligent one.

Only she was not happy in Romania. It was not her country. Then she wanted to go back to Greece and we sent her back. She stayed there for a while, and then Vanghely's wife sent her again back to us.

We had the space, and food was not a problem and she certainly was welcomed to stay with us.

It was Maia who was not happy. It was her eldest son, Tachi, she was thinking of and longing for, the places she knew, and the people she knew.

One vacation we, including Maia, went to Busteni, a beautiful place at the foot of Carpathian Mountains. We set a tent near to a spring and spent the entire summer there camping.The place was beautiful, near the spring and the forest, close enough to the town that we could buy food and necessities, and this way we did not have to spent a lot of money renting a room. Money was tight at that time, with three children in school. My sister and I were at the University, studying to became engineers, and my brother was finishing high school. That was the best we could do for that vacation. We thought is picturesque, and enjoyed the outdoors, cooking over an open fire, and the freedom to stay and sleep outdoors.

It proved fatal for my grandmother.

She got the shingles, maybe from the water we drank, or just plain stress, or cold. No one of us got sick, but her. She got sick when we returned to Bucharest. She got over the shingles, but her immune system weakened from the illness and after a short while she died.

She died saying her eldest son's name-Tacki.

I never figured out exactly how old my grandmother was. When I knew her, she wore long black cloths and had her hair tided up with a black kerchief. She was a tall, proud woman. I supposed the black cloths were for mourning her late husband dead for more than forty years. My mother said that she was in her seventies, but I suspected she was older than that, or maybe she just had a hard life raising the children by herself. She was one of five sisters, and the story goes that she was so beautiful, that her husband stole her from her parents' house when she was only seventeen years old.

At that time and place, women were married for life regardless if the man lived or died. In Avdela divorced was not known, and if a woman strayed she was probably stoned to death. It was all a matter of honor and family pride.

Cristidis

BUCHAREST, ROMANIA, 1970'S

I graduated from the Faculty of Hydrotechnical Constructions with a Master in Science in civil Engineering in 1969. The school, how well I was doing in class, and the grades that I was making were always very important to me. I was so ambitious , so competitive, that a grade less than maximum 10 was a reason for me to start crying. It was not because I doubted my capacities, but because maybe some other students cheated, or used their political clout to get ahead of me and that, I considered an injustice. I never considered cheating. I was in competition mostly with myself and striving for excellence. I was always proving my abilities to myself. But if "they" (meaning the Professors, of course) mistreated me, and maybe gave me a 9+, I felt cheated and humiliated, and when I got home after the exam, I would start crying. Because of the injustice of it, not because I thought I failed in any way. I could not admit failure.

At the University there was only one boy, who, I admitted to myself, was smarter than I. His name was Cristidis, and he was of Greek heritage. His mother had raised him by herself. I do not remember what happened to his father. Cristidis was in love with me, or so he professed, and we went out on dates when we both were in the second year of college. I was not in love with him, even though I admired his intelligence, his seriousness, and his hard work. And of course, it was good to feel and be told that you are loved.

He would wait like a sick puppy dog for me after classes. Cristidis was giving tutoring lessons to younger students and helping his mother make ends meet. He tutored my brother to prepare for the admission to the University. He would come over to our house in that next summer, to tutor my brother, and as my brother said, he would talk only about me.

At his age, he was eighteen years old at the time, Cristidis was helping monetary at home, and helping his mother with the household expenses. It was as if he was the man of the house. His mother was very ambitious for him, and she fully expected him to get his Ph.D. She mapped the road for him. Cristidis was not an ambitious young man, he was simply brilliant. And Cristidis of course, got his Ph. D. very young. He graduated first, in that school year, 1969 promotion, but right next to him, following very close, was I. I did not put the same hard work and seriousness into it, but my intelligence, my talent, and especially my ambition, situated me right behind him, with my total score very close to his. I thought that Cristidis was stronger than me on the abstract subjects, mathematics, physics, the bases of our engineering trade, but when we got to the more specialized courses like Hydraulics, or hydro technical construction I had a quicker understanding of it. The practical and creative part of engineering fascinated me. We both got a 10 on the thesis for the Master's Degree.

Cristidis wanted to marry me, and told me so, but his mother had different plans for him. She wanted him to get his Ph. D degree before he married anybody, and was not ready to release him to any other woman. After graduation I lost track of him. I heard that he got his Ph. D. and became a professor at the same university. During college, we competed fiercely for grades, and I think that was good for me. I do not know if he married later, or not. I think, I heard that he got an ulcer.

The truth be told, I think I would have married Cristidis, if not for his mother! I admired him so much! But then, I did not know about Love!

At the graduation we were supposed to choose our places of employment from a list of available jobs and the order of preferment was the order of the students' final grades. For Cristidis (or rather his mother) was very important to finish the first in class in order to get the only job available as an assistant professor at the university. Even so, I think that somebody else with a political clout took that job away from him that year.

Florin

BUCHAREST, ROMANIA, 1970'S

Upon graduation, my mother advised me to choose the place of employment that was located closer to our home in Bucharest, because the most important thing in life, in her opinion, was that you don't have to travel or spend hours on busses going to and from work. So, I chose a nice-looking place, a beautiful building, situated five minutes walking distance from our house, in the center of Bucharest, on "Calea Victoriei". It happened to be the "Institute of Projection for Mining Industries".

My colleagues over there were older and already established. I was the new kid on the block. They carefully planned my training, and for the first two years I worked with older, more experienced, Engineers and learned the trade, so to speak. It took me longer than my other colleagues to be ready to fly on my own, but when I was ready to take on responsibilities; I flew higher than any of my colleagues. Even the older and more experienced engineers recognized my talent and carefully trained me. For me being and engineer it's not just a job, it is a profession that I passionately love. I love the creativity of it.

The Mining Institute was a place where we planned and design projects for all the mining compounds located all over Romania. We went to those faraway places, in remote mountain locations, and walked to the sites, and visited, and carefully planned for the future developments. We went as a team of engineers of different specialties. My older colleagues were accustomed with those trips, and they took their time, and visited those places, going to nice and picturesque restaurants and taverns while there. It would take us maybe one full week to go to the most remote places, and usually it involved quite a bit of hiking in the hills and mountains.

It was a beautiful time in my life. There I met Florin, who was a young electrical engineer, working for the same Mining Institute. Florin was very handsome and full of life. He was the kind of guy women fall all over. Every woman in that place had a crush on Florin. And he was quite generous with his favors. He believed in living his life to the fullest extent. Unfortunately for me, I fell in love with him. It was not a blind love. I did see Florin's shortcoming and that pained me even more. Florin did not love me, and I knew it. It was an obsession for me of the worst kind. I could not get over it, nor advance the relationship any. I wanted love and could not settle for less. Unfortunately, Florin could not give me love, and I could not admit failure. Everybody at work knew and rooting for me and they were trying to send us together in different places (work related) in hope that we could work out our differences. We could not. Now, that I think back, it was probably because of me, who expected so much out of him and the relationship and could not compromise for less.

Now, looking back, at all the people I knew, and all the flames I had, it occurred to me that I never think of Florin. I often think of other people and men I met over the years, I recall fond memories and joyful events, kind words we exchanged, but never think of Florin.

It is often said that we are put here, on this Earth, for our souls to learn lessons, meet different people and interact with them, in order to grow and enrich our minds and souls form the experiences we have. From every person we meet and interact, we learn a valuable lesson and hopefully they learn something from us in return. For each soul we met in our journey, we leave with them a little piece of our soul, and they do the same with us.

That was not the case with Florin. I did not get anything from him (and I'm <u>not</u> talking about material things, or even physical touch), and I doubted he got anything from me either, as he put up this impenetrable shield around himself. Maybe, behind that shield it was nothing, but my woman intuition was telling me that it was something worth fighting for. I'll never know!

The lesson I learn from my interaction with Florin was that unrequited love is something very painful and degrading to some extent. I never want to think back on it!

* * *

Then the unthinkable happened. The Mining Institute was to be decentralized, divided and established in different regions where the mines were located. We, the employees were to relocate from Bucharest, or to find ourselves another place of employment. I was not willing to move out of Bucharest, and went out and found myself another job, again five minutes walking distance from our house, again located on "Calea Victoriei", at the Institute of Projection for Machine Construction. I was one of the lucky ones. I moved very fast, on my own, went for interviews and tests in other various places and found myself a good job.

Florin went and found himself another job in a different place, and we drifted apart. Later on he married.

* * *

This experience of finding another job, moving fast at my own initiative, proved to be very helpful later on when I was looking for a job in the U.S.

Klaus

MAMAIA, ROMANIA, EARLY 1970'S

Romania has beautiful beaches on the Black Sea. There is its oldest port town Constantza, an international port, hundreds of years old, and there are the relatively new vacation and tourists towns Mamaia, Venus Jupiter, Saturn, etc. There is the students' vacation town Costinesti. Beautiful locations built for vacations and international tourists, with all the new architecture and comforts. Now, that I have been in Greece and seen the beaches over there, and in the U.S. have seen Miami Beaches, and Daytona, and West Palm Beach in Florida, I can say that those vacation locations in Romania were nothing less than what we can see here. There were beautiful hotels on the beaches with all the comforts, with elegant restaurants, shopping centers and gift shops. The beaches were clean and well-kept and the landscapes beautiful. Everything in those new places were built with the idea of attracting the international tourism in Romania. Everything belonged to the government. There were places where access was only for the foreigner tourist, who could afford to spend the hard currency, the dollars.

One summer, just after I finished college, and started my first job, one of my colleagues, Musy, an older married woman, invited some of us to spent a month's vacation in her tent in Mamaia. Musy had this large tent installed in one of the camping area around Mamaia.

The campus itself was well organized. It had cold and hot water showers, restrooms, a grill restaurant, paved alleys and was always occupied at full capacity. That was the affordable way to spent a summer at the beaches. Musy's tent even had a small kitchen and affront porch. She invited me and my friend Doina and another colleague with her husband. The tent had different partitions thus making separate bedrooms. We all had agreat vacation that summer.

My friend Doina was married, but her husband was home in Bucharest studying for some exams. Something was wrong with the marriage because Doina was looking for somebody else. She would not admit it openly, but I could sense it. The married couples were cooking at the tent's kitchen and eating on the tent porch, but Doina and I did not have time for cooking. We wanted to have fun, stay on the beach and not be bothered with cooking. So Doina and I and occasionally the others were having lunch and dinner at the campus grill restaurant. After all, the sleeping arrangements were free. What else we were to spend our money on?

Early one afternoon Doina, Musy and I were having lunch at the grill restaurant when an young blonde handsome man came and asked permission to sit to our table. The young man was German and spoke German. The only one who knew some German was Musy and he started to talk to Musy. He introduced himself as Klaus, and we understood he was from West Germany and was vacationing at the same campus as we. After we were finished with our lunch, Musy invited him to visit us at our tent later on.

In the evening Klaus and his friend from Austria, whom he travel with, came and visited us at Musy's tent, and we had coffee and played music and danced. At the dance it was obvious that Klaus liked me.

The second day we met on the beach and went for long walks and swam. Klaus was a very good swimmer. Later, I found out that Klaus used to run in his Country's Olympic team. I could barely swimm and he would put me on his floating mattress and push me onto the deep waters. I was thinking that I was pretty fortunate this time for not knowing German. We could not speak. Usually my "smarts" and especially my sharp tongue drove men away from me. Or at least that's what I thought.

One evening, Klaus and his Austrian friend invited Doina and me to dance. The place was only for foreigners and the admission was paid only in dollars. That nightclub, back in Romania, at that time, was nothing less than the nightclubs I later visited in the U.S. We had a few drinks and danced all night long. A special kind of bond was forming between Klaus and me. Finally, we discovered that we both knew some French and we could communicate after all. This was the end of August and I had to go back to work. My vacation was ending and Klaus and his friend were continuing their traveling to Turkey, to Istanbul.

Klaus , like many West European youths, had traveled around the globe. We kept writing to each other (in French). In September I was back to Bucharest, and to my engineering job.

One day in September, Klaus walked to my front door in our house in Bucharest, and asked for me. I could not believe my eyes. He was going back to West Germany and had stopped to see me. He stayed with us for about two weeks. My father knew German, and they would talk late into the nights. Klaus would offer to help my mother with the house chores, while I was at work. He was so nice, and so easy to get along with. Finally, he went to Germany and we corresponded.

My birthday is in October, and I remember that when I got home from work that day, a huge bouquet of twenty-one pink roses, my age at the time, was waiting for me. I did not even know that somebody can send flowers from another country. My first thought was that Klaus came back.

The next summer Klaus wrote and invited me and my parents to come and visit him in West Germany. He did not know that this was an impossible thing under the Communist Regime. Nobody could obtain a passport at that time. Maybe I was not ready and lack the courage to depart from my family and fight the authorities to be with Klaus. He would write for many years after that. I even took German lessons and wrote back to Klaus in German.

Many years after that, I kept a dried red bud rose that he gave me, in my closet. I still have his picture in my album. On the back of the picture he wrote: *"Pour moi Grande Amour"*.

When I finally left Romania, and defected in Greece in 1980, the first thing I did was to write to Klaus and try to find him. His address was not the same any longer. I could not trace him back.

All I have from Klaus is a picture, a dried bud rose, a warm remembrance of what could have been, and a book. When he left Klaus gave me a German translation of the book *"The Little Prince"*. It is without doubt the most beautiful book I ever read. First, I read the Romanian translation I found in the Bookstores in Romania, then I read Klaus' book in German, and later I read the English translation of it.

The Earthquake

BUCHAREST, ROMANIA, 1977

Bucharest, as we learned later, it is situated on a"phalli" (earthquakes are caused mostly by rupture of geological faults). That means an earthquake is possible at any time.

In 1977 there was a big earthquake in Romania with its epicenter near Bucharest. I think it was rates as 7.5 on the Richter scale. It was devastating for Bucharest.

I remember on the evening of the earthquake we, the entire family, were watching television. It was around 7:00 p.m. in March.

It was dark outside, and suddenly the bed started to shake, and my father who survived another big earthquake in 1944 in Galati, told us that is was an earthquake. It probably all happened in seconds, but I remember it as in a slow-motion picture. My brother was the first to panic and broke the window with his hand, jumping outside in the yard. Now, the yard in front of that particular window, was very narrow and squeezed between our house and the next house.

Then, my sister jumped out of the window after my brother. Their luck was that the window was at the parterre level, the distance to the ground was just a few feet and of course the adjoining building, or our house, did not collapsed on them. I remember father going toward the front door. He used to tell us that when the earthquake hit Galati he stayed beneath the door frame and that is what we should do in case it ever happened. My mother went to the front door also. I stayed behind and I remember I put out the cigarette butt my brother left behind burning, unplugged the T.V. set, and went toward the front door also. I remember glancing into the front room and seeing the big chine cabinet leaning forward and all my beautiful china vases, set on top of it, exploding. The huge mirror we had on the wall was also leaning forward. It looked like the walls were closing and falling in.

Then, we unlocked the front door and went out in the street. I looked at the sky. It was red; the moon was full and red, looking huge on the sky. It was light as day outside with terrible noise. The people who were in cars, on the street, were moving very carefully, at slow speed. It seemed like everybody was alert and attuned to what was happening around them. I remember, later on they announced on the radio, that no car accidents happened in that night. We probably never before talked to our neighbors, but then, in that evening, and in all days that followed the earthquake, people were talking to each other and showing concern and were ready to help. It was as if we, the people, were these little creatures with no power whatsoever in front of nature and its forces. We all could disappear in a moment from the face of the earth without being able to do anything about it.

We were just crowding together waiting to see what was happening next. We were lucky. Our neighborhood had the majority of its buildings of one-story brick, built very solidly.

The tall buildings in the center of Bucharest were severely affected. More than one multilevel building in the center of town collapsed. They reported something like 1, 200 people dead, but I think the toll was even higher. There were people trapped beneath the rubbish, and teams were working day and night to find them. Some lucky ones were alive, but the majority were dead.

That night, my mother went to the nearby hospital with my brother. He had cut his hand, breaking the window. They were the first victims arriving at the hospital.

There were the army and the firefighters and the volunteers, and people who took off from the office to help clean up the debris and save people trapped under it.

There were terrifying stories about people who were found alive as long as eleven days after the earthquake trapped under the debries.

Our house suffered minor cracks. Few things, porcelain vases, were broken, but nothing major.

Three years later, in 1980 while I was in Greece, there was an earthquake in Athens. Actually, there were a series of earthquakes lasting for about a month. Nothing as devastating as the earthquake in Romania.

Ski Trip

PREDEAL, ROMANIA, 1979

Romania has beautiful ski resorts in the Carpathian Mountains. The ski resorts are very modern and built to attract international tourism to Romania. There are beautiful hotels right on the ski slopes, with indoor swimming pools and saunas and restaurants. There are places one can rent the top of the line ski equipment, and there are *theleski* available in most places.

One winter, while I was working at the Machine Construction Institute in Bucharest, the institute organized a ski trip in Predeal, at a resort located right on the ski slope. It was my first skiing experience. I had no appropriate clothing at the time, and I remember one of my colleagues lending me a red ski jacket and one of them even knitting a peach berretta and a scarf for me. I had ski pants and plenty of woolen sweaters.

The cabin was right on the ski slope. It had a big restaurant, the cafeteria type, downstairs and large women's and men's bedrooms upstairs. We were maybe twenty colleagues from work, spending ten days' vacation skiing.

I rented the skis and the boots from the renting office located right on the slopes. There were good quality skis and hard boots, the one that keeps your ankles locked.

The first day on the slope was terrible. I could not keep my feet from sliding each one in different directions, or myself from falling down on my bottom and not being able to get up. At the end of the first day, I remember that all my muscles were sore and I was hurting all over as if I had been beaten.

The second day, the guys gave me some basic instruction on how to fall down, how to slow down, how to turn. And I started skiing. I had all the courage in the world. I thought that skiing was the most beautiful of all sports and I was willing to learn to master it.

There was guy there, a colleague of mine, who was a very good skier and, seeing my determination to learn and my courage, he offered to help me some. He took me with him on the teleski and told me to ski from the halfway down the slope. First, seeing myself so high on the slope and the slope so abrupt, I froze, but with his expert advice I slowly got down. He told me where to turn and to get from one point to the next the safe way, cutting down the speed. The, I got the knack of it and went up and down the slope by myself. It felt like flying with the wind blowing on my face. I still cannot imagine anything more beautiful than skiing. I was on the slope from morning to dark, and that vacation I learned how to ski pretty well.

On the following ski trip, I was not so lucky. First, I rented the equipment in Bucharest, before leaving in order to save some money. That turned out to be a big mistake. The equipment was a far cry from the equipment I rented on the slope, which was for the tourists. The boots I rented in Bucharest were not the hard high boots but rather short and my ankles, as I found out later, were weak. This time we went to a resort that was located at higher altitude than the first one, a more remote resort, on the top of the mountain. There was plenty of fresh snow on the slopes. This time, the very first time I put the skis on, I fell really badly. The safety gadget on the ski did not open and the ski remained attached to my foot. When I fell, the leg with the ski on, the right leg, bent beneath me and my knee was injured. I could barely walk on that leg, but I stayed for the remaining of the vacation. Then when I went back to Bucharest, and back to my work limping, the same colleague who knitted my ski cap, took me to the hospital. The doctor said I injured my meniscus and put my entire leg in a cast. The cast came off in about ten days, but afterwards I had a hard time bending the leg, and even staying in a chair at my office's desk. Gradually the leg and the knee healed.

I still hope to have another opportunity to go skiing. I still dream of being able to ski.

I think I learned my lesson. You need to be in excellent physical form, you need to have the top of the line equipment, and you need a good coach, at least in the beginning.

But nothing can be more beautiful than skiing.

Easter In Daddy

GREECE, 1980

Back in 1980's I spent one year in Greece, waiting to get my entrance visa for the Unites States. I have relatives from my mother side living in Greece. I didn't have to stay at "*Latrium*" the refugee campus located just outside Athens, Greece. From the stories I heard circulating within the immigrant community, I consider myself very lucky that I did not have to stay there. There is always a price you need to pay for your freedom. In my case, I had to fend for myself and earn my living for the entire time I stayed in Greece-fourteen months. But my fondest memories are from the time I spent alone in Greece with no formal obligations to anybody, with time in my hands, for the first time in my life with no strict working and office hours.

One memorable time of Easter comes in mind. My relatives had a vacation house in Daddy, the village where my uncle's wife came from. The village was outside Athens about two hours by buss, in the hills. I remember the village with its houses rising from the valley where the open market *"Platia"* was, to the hills and wondering along the white, stony, narrow alleys. Some of the houses were rebuilt and completely modernized by the people living now in Athens, who used them for weekend's retreats and vacations; some others were the original village houses with its inhabitants.

The entire village looked white—streets, alleys paved with white river stones, houses all painted in white, the sun shining bright, as in no other place on earth, the sky incredible blue. The village had two platias: one on the lower level plateau where the annual fair took place and where all the shops were located and another one on the higher level plateau where there was a small fountain in the middle and a coffee shop on the corner. Invariable, every time I passed by, old men would sit at the outside table and drink strong Greek coffee from small finger like cups with side glasses of ice water. The men would finger a string of beads called "kubuloi". They were supposed to say a prayer for each bead, every time they fingered the beads.

My uncle's house was high on the hill, built upon the foundation of an old house. The basement of the old house was used as the foundation and big great room was built in top of it. The kitchen, the small bedroom and the lavatory were part of the old house. To get to the house, you had to climb a steep alley.

Atop the highest part of the village, on the hill, there was the church, all white with great stone walls, adorned with "icons" framed in silver and gold.

My uncle and I got to the village on Thursday of the Holy Easter Week. On Good Friday, we dressed up and went to the church around 7:00 P.M. The entire village was there. The women of the village had decorated the "patrafiriu" beautifully with fresh flowers. Around 9:00 P.M. the *prohod* was formed, headed by the priest, the altar boys caring the Holy Cross, then the *patrafiriu* carried by four devoted men, followed by the entire population of the village holding candles. The entire *prohod* was outside the church headed toward the middle town *Platia*. There, by the fountain, the priest stopped, they put down the *patrafiriu* and started the Friday night services. The entire community was outside, under the stars around the *patrafiriu*, each person holding a lighted candle in hand. The spectacle was breathtaking, with the people arranged as in an amphitheater. When the priest finished the services, he gave each person a flower from the *patrafiriu* to take home with them.

The following day, Saturday morning, the people who kept Lenten vows and fasted, according to the laws of the church, went for communion.

My uncle had ordered a whole young lamb, about twenty pounds, from the village butcher and we went to pick it up on Saturday morning. The butcher had already slaughtered the skinned the lamb and cleaned it up for us. On Saturday the people cleaned up their houses and finished preparation for the Easter night feast. By the early evening, we are awaiting guests to pass by the house and wish us a happy Easter. The treat for the gusts was a bowl of Turkish delights. In the evening around 12:00 A.M., again the entire village was at the Church to receive the Light and the Holy Easter and afterward to bring the lighted candles home, bringing the Holy Light within their homes.

Sunday morning, very early, the men of the village were setting up fires, maybe a big fire for each plateau for three to four households. By the time I woke up, the fires were smoldering, and each family had their fresh cut lamb on a stick on top of the red charcoals, roasting. The women of the houses prepared inside the houses a meal made with the lamb inwards called "maghiritza" and were coming out to the places where men were roasting the lambs, and treating all of them with "maghiritza" and wine. By the time the lamb was completed roasted, everybody had their fill of food and wine.

Later on the day, my uncle's son, Iani, came over and prepared the traditional "cucuretzi".This is done from pieces of meat and onions, stringed on a stick and tied up with the lamb intestines (well cleaned up in advance). These were roasted over the charcoals and eaten on the spot. There were also dyed eggs and "zureche" –the Eastern bread.

Sunday at lunch we were expecting guests from Athens to share the Easter feast. For them it was like a regular pic-nick outside the big City. It takes a closer look and involvements with the village people's life to really get an inside look at the customs.

I returned to Greece from U.S.A. in 1983 and then back in 1986 and found the same people unchanged by time or world's events. The same old men drinking coffee at the coffee shop with the *kumburloi* in their hands. Same people talking about the same things, three and then six years later.

The Greek people consider themselves as godly, therefore perfect and in no need of any change.

Maria Giftaki

GREECE, 1980

Now, that I think back every woman who touched my life, in a good sense of the word, was named Maria. Maybe I'm just presumptuous to believe that Maria-the Mother of Jesus Christ- is my Protector.

First time I met Maria Giftaki (Giftacki in the Greek Language means –gypsy) when she visited us in Romania back in 1970's. Maria was the ex-wife of my mother's cousin, Kotchiu. Maria was a beautiful woman, with passionate dark eyes and black hair. The entire time she visited with us, she talked about Kotchiu and how they separated because of his political beliefs. Kotchiu was one of those people who really believed that life can be changed for the better, and dedicated his entire life and his family fortune to the "cause", the "Communist cause" to be more precisely. Maria had different beliefs and was not willing to sacrifice her life or money for the "cause". She loved Kotchiu dearly and never really got over him, but she would not follow him in his underground activities. She did not believe in the "cause".

Maria was visiting Romania and all of Kotciu's relatives because in her heart, he still was her husband, till the day she died. I never witnessed such passion, such force and deepness of feeling until I met Maria.

When I went to Greece, in 1980, Maria was probably in her late sixties, but she had the heart of a young girl. She would call Kotchiu on the phone, just to hear his voice and then hung up. She would send me, as his relative, to visit Kotchiu at the hospital when he was ill, and sent him sweets.

When I was living in Greece, waiting for my visa to enter the US, Maria and her family helped and sustained me morally and emotionally throughout the entire ordeal.

Of course, I had my mother's relatives, but they treated me with coldness. They did what was expected of them, but beneath it, I could feel the coldness, the indifference. And it was a very difficult time for me. I was there alone, apart from my family for the first time in my life, without knowing the language, without much money, without knowing what was going to happen to me next.

For the first two months of my stay in Greece, I lived with my relatives, but afterward they let me know that I have overstayed my welcome and it was time that I found a "garsoniera" for myself and moved out. My cousin, Marula-Tachi's daughter, helped me find a "garsoniera" for rent, lent me a folding bed, a shabby table and a chair, and washed her hands of me. There I was, living on my own for the first time in my life. The problem was that I had to pay the rent, and the utilities, and buy food for myself, when I had not legal right to work in Greece, and had very little money. I also didn't know the Greek language and had to deal with the Authorities to solve the problems about my departure.

Maria and her sister Pipitza, and Pipitza's children treated me as if I was a part of their family. Every time I went and vested Maria, she would receive me with open arms. She would listen to all my problems, and gave me strengths to get through. She taught me about religion and church. I learned Greek, speaking with her and with Tereza and Pipitza.

At Maria's I watched television, and drank coffee, and found an oasis of Love among strangers.

I remember visiting Maria's And Pipitza's family when they were on summer vacation and rented a flat at Vuliagmeni, on the Mediterranean Sea, near a thermal spring.

Maria had introduced me to Mimis, who owned an engineering construction company, in hope that I will find employment. She was the one who went with me at the Ministry of Education to translate my diploma. She was the one who took care of me when I got sick with a broken heart over Costas. They just received me and accepted me as one of them. I was invited to lunches and spent days visiting with the family in Vuliagmeni. I felt like I belonged.

Later on, when I moved to the USA, I got a chance to repay some of my moral debt to Maria. She needed an eye operation and I brought her to have her surgery here. But I don't think I could ever repay the goodness and love she gave me.

Costas

GREECE, 1980.

Maria Giftaki introduced me to Mimis, in order for me to find employment. Mimis' mother was a good friend and colleague of Maria's sister Pipitza. They had known each other for years, as Mimi's mother and Pipittza were both teachers at same school. Maria thought that Mimis had a moral obligation toward their family, as once, Mimis' mother along with her young boy were strangers in Athens and Maria had helped them get established. Mimis owned an engineering contracting company in Athens and I was an engineer.

One early evening, I went to Mimis' company and talked to him and his employees. My Greek at that time was very poor. I could understand what was said, but I could not speak the language yet. I also spoke some English at the time, and my English was improving, as I was taking classes at Hellenic-American Institute in Athens. I don't know exactly how well Mimis had understood my Greek or my English, but he understood that I was in desperate need for help and that reminded him of his early years when he and his mother were poor and in need of help too. Then Maria and Pipitza and their family helped them. Now,

Mimis was quite well off. Mimis was married at the time to a woman who used to be referred to as the "Monster" because she was ugly. But that woman was rich, when Mimis was poor, and her money had helped him get started.

He was talking about getting a divorce, but he had second thoughts because of his daughter. He did not want to do any harm to the child by getting a divorce. Meanwhile, as I could observe, he had plenty of affairs with his girlfriends.

Mimis asked me if I used to work in construction or design, and we agreed that probably I was looking for employment with a consulting company. Later on, he found a job for me with a consulting company who worked with his construction company doing design.

That first evening, Mimis told me about knowing somebody who would make a good husband for me, Costas, as my first desire was to get married and establish myself in Greece (that being the only legal way I could remain in Greece). Costas was also an engineer and worked for Mimis on occasions.

The working hours in Athens were like this: first they worked from eight in the morning to noon. At noon everybody went home for lunch and a nap , or "siesta" as it's known in all those Mediterranean countries; then when the temperature cooled off some, in the afternoon around 4:00 P.M., they would go back to work and work to maybe 6:00 P.M. Then, they started talking about where to go for the evening and always ended up going to a restaurant or "buzuchia".

One has to understand that work in Greece was almost exclusively a men's world. If a woman got married, she would no longer work. A woman was not expected to have an education or to be able to hold down a job. All that was expected of her, it was to get married. In order to get married, a woman had to have "prika" or dowry. The usual dowry, for a girl to marry well, was a house. Her husband would provide for her and the family. In return, she would cook and take care of the house and raise children and basically not interfere with the man's world. He was free to go out to restaurants and have a good time. The wife was supposed to stay home and wait. Usually the wife would wait home with the food warm in the oven and would not even ask where the husband was.

From this perspective, Greece and the Greek people's mentality were hundreds of years behind, even Romania. I was raised in Communist Romania where women were perfectly equal to the men and everybody was obliged to work, by law. Therefore, there want not even a shred of doubt in my mind that I was less equal to a man in my profession as an engineer, or that I would not have the same responsibilities and freedom as a man. I was working in a men dominated profession and always thought to be right at the top of it.

Mimis would take me with them when they were visiting construction sites and give me the opportunity to visit different sites of Greece, which otherwise I would not have had the resources to visit on my own. We would stop at small restaurants on the sea shore and eat fresh fish, or shrimp, or even a just caught octopus, things that were new to me.

However, there was always somebody else with us, and at no time did Mimis make a pass at me or give me the impression that maybe, he had different thoughts other than friendly. After all Mimis was a married man.

One evening, Mimis invited me to his office, and introduced me to Costas and afterward we, the employees, went out to "bouzuchea". This was the first time I was to a "bouzuchea" and I was very impressed. I remember they had a "diseuse" and the food was excellent. I heard before stories of rich people going there and having fun and throwing the dishes on the floor and the glasses in the fire place after the party was over (that is for good luck!). But what impressed me was Costas. He was tall and handsome and soft-spoken and well-educated. Costas had studied in England and was very sophisticated (or at least that's what I thought).I liked him very much from the beginning, and I thought he liked me as well. So, I started dating Costas, talking to him over the phone a lot, and going out. I was getting fonder of him. But the time for me to leave Greece was approaching fast.

One weekend, toward the end of my stay in Greece, Mimis had invited me to spend the weekend with his family in Raffia. Raffia was a summer resort on the Mediterranean Sea about two hours by bus from Athens. So, early Friday afternoon, I took the bus and went to Raffia. Mimis owned this new fifteen-to-twenty-story building right on the beach. I thought the building was worth a fortune. His wife and his friends were preparing for a party that evening. They were talking about a "proxenia", which means they were introducing a woman to a man with the idea of a possible marriage. As the evening progressed, I heard the women mentioning the name "Costas". There were preparations taking place. Mimi's mother and a lot of other guests were there. They all arrived in their cars. Probably, I was the only one to get there by bus. The young girl to be introduced, the "nefi", meaning bride, was already there, and the women were fussing around her to get her to look her best.

About eleven o'clock, the "gambrol", meaning the groom, showed up. To my utter despair, it turned out to be none other than Costas. My Costas. I thought I would be violently sick. I remember starting to tremble, and Mimis' wife brought me a sweater, thinking that I was probably cold. I found myself trapped there, in the middle of strangers, with no way of escaping the trap. I could not leave in the middle of the night. The busses were not circulating at that hour.

Costas behaved as if he did not know me. I did not want to give satisfaction to Mimis by showing how badly I hurt, and I talked to one of the guests and convinced him to take me back to Athens, under the illusion that I was interested in him. Of, course, after he got me to my house, he never heard from me again.

The next day I went to Maria in Vuliagmeni and was sick in bed for a week.

It has been a long time since I got over Costas, but Mimis cruelty I still remember.

Why Mimis arranged this, I cannot understand to this day. Maybe he just wanted to show me the real face of Costas, not the pretty one that everyone could see, but the cowardly one that I could not see for myself. Maybe, Mimis, in his own way was telling me to move on, as it was nothing there for me.

On the other hand, maybe Mimis had designs of his own on me and was frustrated because could not act on it.

ATHENS, GREECE, 1980.

When my cousin, Marula, understood that I had to stay perhaps a longer time in Greece and I had problems getting my papers ready, she decided she could not keep me any longer, as a gust in her house. She was married and had two small children. She had enough on her shoulders already, without me.

Then, she told me that I have to find myself a place to rent and move out. I was very distressed at the time and did not know where to go and how I was going to survive in a foreign country without knowing the language, without resources, and without the legal right to work. I supposed I was hanging onto her for my dear life, but as it turned out, it was the best thing ever to happen to me. It gave me a chance to rapidly grow up and stand on my own two feet.

Back in Romania, I was living with me family, and my parents had always sheltered us. I was old enough, but still had the attitude of a small child. It was the first time in my life I was on my own.

Marula went with me, and we were looking for a "garsoniera" to rent. The "garsoniera" was an efficiency apartment with one bedroom, a small kitchen and a bathroom. All that we looked at, in my price range, were terrible looking, depressing places, and I could not imagine myself living there.

Finally, we found a place nearby, at the foot of "Licavithos" in a nice building. The garsoniera was on the first floor of the building. It was very clean, full of sunlight gleaming hardwood floors and a small balcony facing the street. I was very happy. I ran to Maria and to my uncle and borrowed the money to pay two month's rent. Then I met Tereza's mother, the owner of the building, who told me that her daughter, Tereza, was a very good woman and she will help me get established.

Marula got me a folding bed, a table, and a chair and that was the end of it. She never got back to visit me, or to ask how I was doing.

I clean up the place, set up the bed, the table and chair, and brought fresh-cut flowers from the open market nearby. I brought a little kerosene stove and a small pan and I was set. As far as I was concerned, if I had a way to make coffee, that was everything I needed. I was never so happy in my life. Now, I could close the door, and do what I liked the most- reading actually. I was reading English novels, because I couldn't read Greek-they have a different alphabet, not the Latin root one like Romanian, or English, or French.

I did not have a job at the time, so I was free to go to the beaches and walk and visit places I had never gone to before. I had a little problem though. I had to come up with the money to pay the rent and utilities at the first of the month and buy a minimum of food for me. Believe it or not, I managed to do that for one full year. I was living on $100 a month without having the feeling that I was missing anything. I paid $50 a month in rent and maybe another $10 for water and electricity and the rest I used to buy food and bus tickets and pay the admission to the beaches. I had beautiful cloths from back in Romania and my mother sent me my bed linens. I invested in a sheer curtain for the French door leading to the balcony and a blanket for my bed. My mother was sending by the Greek students' buss "kasseri" and dry salami I could keep without having to refrigerate it. I didn't have a refrigerator and could not buy any perishable food. I was going every Saturday morning to the "laiki", the neighborhood open market.

Each Saturday morning, the farmers from around Athens would open a market in each neighborhood. I would buy fresh eggs and potatoes, and green salad, and lemons and oranges. My dayly meal was fried eggs and French fries that I could cook on the kerosene stove. Then I would have melba toast with honey in the mornings with my coffee. I would eat my fill every Sunday at lunch, when my uncle Vangheli would have me at his house, and every time I was invited at lunch or dinner by my friends. I simply used to take the bus, almost every morning, and go visit all the beaches near Athens. Every day I would go to a different place, as far as the bus would take me. I visited Glifada, where the Americans were located, Vula, and Vuliagmeni, and Sonio. The bus route to the beaches was beautiful, meandering along the high Coast of the Mediterranean Sea. The sky was blue, incredible blue, and the sea was the same shade of blue, reflecting the sky.

I do not remember ever raining in Greece. I had to pay a nominal fee to access the beaches, but they were kept very clean. They were equipped with changing cabins, showers, restaurants and chairs and umbrellas on the beaches.

Then, in the afternoons, I went window-shopping. Athens had the most incredible jewelry shops; hand crafted 18 carat gold jewels with beautiful settings and designs. Then, there was "Ermou" Street, where all the designer cloths and exclusive boutiques were located. One could easily spend a day just window-shopping. I walked all over Athens and came to know it better than Bucharest. I remember one time when I blew, a month's rent to have my hair done at "Alexander", the exclusive salon for the rich. Then I struggled to pay the next month's rent.

To me everything was new, and like a wonderful adventure. I did not mind the hardship.

Of course, there were people who helped me, but not with money, not even as much as a penny, not even my relatives. The money I had to earn it myself. My mother used to send me by bus (the Greek students' bus that was traveling between Athens and Bucharest almost every week and was serving the Greek students who were studying in Bucharest) different china services, that I sold in Athens to earn money, at least in the beginning. The job of selling was not easy. I had to carry those heavy plates to different places and show them to a lot of people and try to sell them when all the shops and their windows were filled with beautiful things.

Later on, I got an engineering job, with Maria's and Mimis' help.

I never complained, and the crazy thing was that I was the one to give presents and gifts to everybody and they accepted them, and even more they expected them, as if I was rich and they were poor. Nobody was asking if I had the money to pay the rent, or what I was eating, or if I had a bed cover for the winter. Mother had to call my uncle and told him to give me a "flocata", so I have something warm to cover myself during the winter.

Tereza was the co-owner, together with her mother, of the building I was living in. Tereza was married to an engineer who worked for the telephone company. At that time he was working in another city for the entire duration of my stay in Greece, I never met him. They had a daughter, Rania, in school.

Tereza had studied in Germany together with her husband. She knew German and Greek Literature, and was giving private lessons to children, out of her home, both in German and Greek Literature. That and the rent on the apartments in her half of the building was her way of making a living. Her husband was not sending her or the child any money. From what I heard, he found himself another woman, where he worked. Tereza was devastated by this fact and was trying to cope with it the best she could, which was not very well. She started drinking. I noticed that she would start drinking in the morning and drink all day long, not enough to make her look like she was drunk, but she drank constantly.

She was as her mother said, a very good and generous woman. She introduced me to Mr. Lavranos, a lawyer friend of hers, and they both looked after my paperwork for the Greek Government. Tereza's greatest hope was to help me to remain in Greece, but it turned out this was not possible. I was Romanian after my father, even though I was born in Greece. I think that, from her perspective, she was happy to have a friend, to be able to talk to about her husband and the great love for him. I was happy to have a friend too. She was very smart and educated, and her family was one of the best in Athens. Her father used to be a General and she knew a lot of important people.

I remember the time when we went to Licavithos. Licavithos is a mountain, rather a hill, in the middle of Athens. Tereza's house was located at the foot of the hill. From my window I could see the mountain and the lights in the evening. There were two restaurants at two different levels, an open theater, and at the top of the mountain there was a small church, "Aghios Dimitrios". We went on foot, but a lot of other people were driving right to the top of the mountain. The view from the top, especially in the evenings, was breathtaking-the whole city below the mountain with its street lights, traffic lights, and houses lightened. Tereza knew the owner of one of the two restaurants.

She also knew the good places to eat around Athens, those places called "tavernas", not luxurious, but with the best food. The tables were not set with white linens, but rather with white and red checkered paper tablecloths, and the general aspect of those places were rustic, but the food was excellent.

We had some other good times, me, Tereza, Rania and her mother.

I went back to Greece from the U.S.A. in 1983 and then in 1986. This time Tereza's husband was around, and he was all right, really. Tereza was still drinking and taking herself into an early grave.

Why do the best of us, the most intelligent, the most sensitive and good hearted people, end up like that?

Peggy

JACKSONVILLE, FLORIDA, U.S.A. 1981.

At the end of summer 1981, I was in Athens, Greece waiting to find a sponsor to be able to enter the U.S.A.

I was on the World Churches' list and already approved by the American Embassy to enter the Unites States as an immigrant.

The only thing needed for my departure was to find a sponsor in the U.S.A. Some people had relative, others had friends, others who did not know anybody, were on the waiting list, and different Churches in the U.S.A. would sponsor them. Usually , the quickest way was for each individual to find his or her own sponsor.

One day I was in my uncle's pastry shop in Omonia, Athens, when a lady entered the shop. She was very tanned, wearing a lot of jewelry, and also wearing short shorts, which was not permitted in Athens. Only the tourists wore shorts in Athens. Her name was Kiki, and she used to work for my uncle maybe twenty years back. She was now an America, married with an American service man, and established in Jacksonville, Florida. She was visiting her relatives in Greece that summer and stopped to say hello to my uncle. There I was, with my problem of finding a sponsor, and my uncle brought up the problem of my sponsorship to Kiki.

Kiki said right on the spot that she would do it, and gave me her address in the U.S.A. She took all my data from me then and there. The entire meeting was something like ten to fifteen minutes and after a while I totally forgot about it.

Meanwhile, my mother wrote me from Romania with the name and address of one of her relatives, a first cousin established in New York City. I wrote him a nice letter asking him to sponsor me. This man, who was a high school teacher at that time, replied with a nice letter and told me that he would contact the World Churches organization in N.Y. for me. We corresponded in English. I was very happy and started to prepare for my departure to the U.S.A. I brought some navy sacks from "Monastirachi" the Athens open market, and started to pack all my belongings in those navy sacks (the kind that seaman are using) and then sewed them up neatly. I accumulated quite a bit of stuff, with what my mother sent me from Romania and what I had in Greece. I made some really good packages and was ready to go whenever I would receive the air plane ticket from the organization. My contact with the other Romanian refugee that were waiting to immigrate to the U.S.A., or Canada, or Australia, was minimal. It was a rough time for all of us and everybody was doing their best to survive. Nobody but me was alone though, they had their families with them.

Finally they notified me from the organization that my papers were ready and that I need to pass the physical examination. After that I received the airplane ticket.

I went and bid farewell to all the people I knew in Athens and called for a taxi to take me to the airport. I went by myself, as I came by myself, all alone. I did not expect anybody to go with me at the airport therefore, I was not disappointed.

I made a pact with myself not to think of what would happen to me in America. If I was to think on the subject, I would be afraid and lack to courage to go forward. It was like taking a big plunge, head first falling down in a bottomless pit. If I started thinking, I would get butterflies in my stomach. I did not know what would happen to me. Somehow, I think I put my life in God's hands and refused to dwell on it. It happened to be the best thing I could possible do, because God was looking out for me. Of all the horrible things that could have happened, and did happen to other people, I was lucky. I met only wonderful people and my life opened up like a flower. Somehow I never expected less. I never thought that anything bad could happen to me. I made a conscious effort to get all the negative thoughts and fears out of my mind. And it worked. All those positive thinking technics that I came to read about later on I applied without knowing what I was doing, and they worked.

In the airplane, was another Romanian family going to Orlando, Florida, to some of their relatives. At that time I was convinced I was going to New-York to stay with my uncle.

When we arrived in New-York, at the Kennedy Airport, the people from the Church Organization were at the airport and gave me a ticket to Jacksonville, Florida. I was astonished. I had totally forgotten about Kiki, and Jacksonville. I had not much time to argue, or be distressed, because I had to catch the airplane to Atlanta then change planes to Jacksonville. All this was new to me and I did not know if I could handle it on my own with so much luggage. Nobody was available to baby-sit me, though. The air plane attendants told me that I was doing just fine with my English and nobody would take me for an immigrant. I could speak English and ask intelligent questions and get oriented fairly easy. In Atlanta I change planes and went to Jacksonville, Florida. Kiki and her husband were waiting for me at the airport, and took me over to their house in Jacksonville Beach. It was 2:00 A.M. It seemed to me like an interminable trip. I arrived in the U.S.A. on September 29, 1981.

Kiki's house was large enough to house a guest. She had three bedrooms and two baths. Her two teenage daughters agreed to share the same bedroom and offered me the other. Kiki and her husband were working from dawn to night. Their daughters were attending school.

I remember the first night in Kiki's house after everybody had retired for the night. I found myself in a foreign country, I did not know anything about, among strangers I have not seen in my life, cut off from my family in Romania, and even my relatives in Greece. That night, alone in my bed, I got scared. I felt cut off from all my roots and quite alone in the world. As the dawn approached I could hear noises of construction work nearby, and then I felt at home, that no matter where I am on the globe, people are the same, and I'm part of them.

The next day, Kiki took a day off from her job, and we went to the Immigration office and I got my social Security Number. Kiki also told me that in about ten day her and her family is planning to move back to Greece. Her husband was retiring from the Navy after the mandatory twenty years of service and they plan to sell the house and move to Greece. Her promise to my uncle back in Greece was that she would prepare the legal forms for me and keep me ten day after my arrival, not more. She kept her promise and I respect her for that.

We called my uncle in New-York and Kiki asked him to take me because she was supposed to move pretty soon. My uncle gave her the run-around, not saying openly that he had no intention of doing anything, but Kiki who was a very sharp woman, understood. She told me to forget about him, because he was not going to help me any. He offered just excuses. She told me to find somebody who would help me. She introduced me to Maria, A Greek lady who used to have breakfast at the place where Kiki was working as a waitress.

Maria turned out to be my salvation. She opened the right doors for me. She kept me at her house for about a week after Kiki left and then introduced me to her friend Peggy.

Peggy was a nurse working for the navy, and at the time, she was looking for a roommate. She was single, about my age, and she owned a house in Mandarin.

Peggy took me to stay at her house. I stayed at Peggy's for two month without having to pay for anything. I did not have anything. Meanwhile, I found a job as an Engineer with the Department of Environmental Protection in Jacksonville, found an apartment, brought a car, got my driver's license, and by the end of December 1981, I was all set.

Maria, Peggy and I became good friends and later shared good times over lunches, dinners and dinner parties. We traveled to New-York and visited my uncle. We visited Washington, D.C. and Maria pushed me through the door of Congressman Bill Chappel, to help me bring my family over.

Maria was going through a painful divorce at the time after thirty years of marriage. She still had two younger children living at home, a home that she was not sure she would be able to keep.

Maria opened the doors for me and helped me get established. She could not do anything for her son or even her daughter, or for my family later on, but she surely helped me.

Congressman Bill Chappel

WASHINGTON D.C., 1982.

After I established myself in Jacksonville, Florida, I started to work diligently to bring my family over from Romania. The understanding I had with my family when I left Romania in 1980, was that I would help them get out of Romania, too.

For me, it was a sacred obligation. It was simply something I had to do no matter what or how. I knew I could not live my live and be content with myself until I fulfilled my promises to my family.

Back, in Romania, under the Ceausescu Regime, things were rapidly getting worse. The food shortage was getting even worse than at the time I was there. Mother had to spend the entire day waiting in line to get some meat, or eggs, or even bread. As my family wrote to me in 1982, 1983, 1984, or 1985, the government issued *"chartels"* to buy sugar or cooking oil. That means there was a certain ratio for each individual, something like a half kilogram of sugar per person per month, nothing more. (I know it sounds like a lot of sugar for people here, in the U.S., who is trying to lose weight, but over there it was one of the main cooking ingredients). They had to stay in line and fight with other people to get propane gas for the stove and heating fuel for the house in winter time. (In Romania there were not electric stoves and central air and heat like here in the U.S., and winters were pretty cold).

Everything was grey, the streets, the houses, the people and their heavy cloths, the people's faces were grey. Nobody was smiling on the streets. Everybody was hurrying about their businesses walking with their heads hung down.

After I defected from Romania, under the pretense of visiting my relatives in Greece, and did not return, my family was interrogated by the police and secret service. My mother told them that probably I got married in Greece and never came back, and that was the extent of the statement from my family about my departure. The government took over the ownership of my part of the big house (one half of it) and my family had to pay rent for using it. The situation became unbearable for my family. I knew I had to do something and pretty soon.

My family backed me up 100 percent while I stayed in Greece. Without my mother sending me things to sell and food, I would never have made it.

Now it was my term to do something for them.

But bringing them over to the U.S.A. was quite an impossible thing, as I soon found out. I went to everybody: to the Archbishop of the Greek Orthodox Church, to the Lutheran Services here in Jacksonville, To Immigration, to the Labor Department. The answer was the same. I would be able to bring them over in six years after I got my American Citizenship.

In the fall of 1982, Maria, Peggy, and I went to visit New-York and Washington, D.C. There in Washington, Maria literally pushed me though the door to Congressman Bill Chappel, the Fourth District Congressman for Jacksonville, Florida.

I walked directly from the street into his office without having an appointment. Yet, he received me. I remember sitting in this great room across from the congressman and telling him my story. Then I made my plea for help. I knew, right there, in that moment, just by looking in his eyes that this man would help me, that he would do whatever was necessary to resolve my problem. He had deep-set, kind, and understanding eyes, which saw a lot of unhappiness in his life.

It took a while and a lot of correspondence with Congressman Chappel's stuff in Washington D.C., and here, in Jacksonville, in the local office, but finally he solved the problem for me. At the American Embassy, in Romania, my family got visas to come to the Unites States. It was the end of 1983, when my family told me they got the visas.

In that year, in December 1983, I brought a house and prepared it to receive my family. It was a small house, nothing like the house we had in Romania, but I thought we would have a roof over our heads.

It was February 1986, when my family finally got here.

My father had died in December 1985. It was strange, as if they could not leave until my father had died. My father was very patriotic and loved Romania very much. Romania was his country.

* * *

After the fall of the communist Regime in Romania, and when I first got a chance to travel back to Bucharest, in summer of 2001, I brought my father's ashes with me in the air plane and bought him a resting place here, in Jacksonville. We are now all together.

* * *

I did not know my father was not coming until the last minute. My mother thought to spare me the grief for a while. But when I heard the news just days before their arrival, I was devastated.

My mother did not like the house I brought and she pushed me until I bought an older home near the center of Jacksonville, in an old neighborhood, Saint Marco, a house that reminded her of our house back in Romania.

I met Congressman Bill Chappel, again in 1987, when he came to Jacksonville for his reelection campaign. Both my sister and I worked in his reelection campaign. Unfortunately, he did not get reelected that time. I remember my sister and I going to a party he gave at his residence in Keystone, Florida, after the elections. Hundreds of people from all over his District, all ages and professions were there. At that time, I did not know that he battled bone cancer, and he was silently fighting for his life. I remember people getting up and talking about how the congressman touched their lives and helped them. I remember, my wanting to get there, in front of all those people and tell them my story, how the congressman had helped me. But, I lacked the courage.

I regret it to this day. The event was a tribute paid to a great man, the rare kind who makes American History and America the Nation that it is today.

A New Life

JACKSONVILLE, FLORIDA 1980'S

After my arrival I worked diligently to establish myself in Jacksonville, Florida. I had a good job with the State of Florida, probably the best job I ever had, but I did not know that at the time. My salary was not very high, just enough for me to cover my apartment's rent and utilities, pay for my car expenses, buy food for myself and have a good time with my friends. There was not much left over, for savings, after that. I was constantly trying to save money. In the back of my mind, I knew that my family would come soon and would need some savings to help them get started. I was in a continuous fight with myself and my tendency for overspending, because there was not much money left to save, after I paid all my bills.

My first job was an engineering job, but not a professional engineering (P.E.) job. For that I had to pass the two full days of state license examination. That was the only way to better my employment opportunities and my earnings capabilities. As soon as I found out about the state license exam, I made up my mind to do it, and as soon as possible. My friend, Kathleen, who worked with me for the state, and who helped me get an apartment in the same complex where she lived, told me about the professional engineer's examination. I arrived in the U.S.A. on September 29, 1981, and started to work on November 24, 1981. In January of 1982, I started the refresher courses for the P.E. examination , that the Florida Engineering Society, Local Chapter, was offering.

I barely knew how to drive, and the classes were offered in Downtown, late in the evenings. That did not stop me. In October of 1982, I went to Tampa, Florida, and took both days of the examination and passed one of them. Then, in April 1983, I passed the other day of the examination. By April of 1983, I received the notification form the Florida Board of Professional Engineers, that I was a licensed P.E. in the State of Florida. At that moment, I started to look for a better place of employment, to correspond with my new title. Kathleen told me then that the state job was the best and most secure job she ever had. The extra time and fixed hours schedule, the security and the pension plan made up for the additional money I could receive in private industry. I would not listen. I wanted the money and the glory and the challenge. I wanted to test my capacities and see how far I could go. Until then, everything had unfolded really easy at my feet, just for trying it and asking it. That's not entirely true, of course. It was my determination and my hard work, behind my every success.

In the beginning, at my state job, I had my dictionary next to me on the desk, and looked up every word I could not understand (I had to enforce, therefor completely understand, the Florida laws). The other big, stepping stone, for me, was the writing of legal documents and letters in English. The fact that I was foreign born, was not an excuse for poor communication skills. I had to be at the level that was required for my job, and be the best at it. My secretary and my boss have helped me in my struggles with the English language. I was to verify and give permits to the consulting engineers in Jacksonville, apply the State statues, and be able to communicate efficiently both orally and in writing. That was essential for my job.

I also had to overcome my lack of driving experience and the fact that I was not familiar with the Jacksonville and surrounding areas.

Altogether, I had six car accidents, until I finally learn to drive safely. But I would not let any of that stop me. I was determined to do my absolute best, and go as far as my abilities would take me.

I had good friends, Maria and Peggy, and we would spend a lot of time together. Something was missing, though. I craved a romantic relationship. All my life I was waiting for it. I was ready for it. Now, both Maria and Peggy, and a lot of my other girlfriends were single and looking for the "right man". Someone, a man, told me, that in Jacksonville there were six women for each man. That was the general ides: men were hard to find and even harder to keep, as Maria knew very well.

I was working with practically every engineer, and sometimes contractors in Jacksonville, checking their work for compliance with the state laws.

It all started gradually and innocently enough. After all "M" was married. He was wearing his wedding ring, and getting involved with a married man was something that was <u>not</u> in my agenda. I wanted to get married. This man, though, was charming and always complimenting the way I looked, the way my hair was arranged, or the cloths I was wearing. He paid attention to me and make me feel like a woman and a woman to be desired. Now, maybe that was the way he was with all women. He appreciated beautiful women, like he appreciated good food, or a good drink, or the good things in life. It started with work, and me admiring his intellect and his engineering abilities, and him admiring my mind and my intellectual capabilities.

It started at the Greek Festival here in Jacksonville. The Greek Orthodox Church was holding its annual Greek Festival in town, and I was working at the festival, cooking and serving food and having fun.

Saturday evening, I was there with my friends and met him and his wife. We all stayed at one table, and had Greek food and " Mavrodafi", Greek wine. I was dancing the Greek dances and had drunk too much of the sweet wine. I was getting tipsy. That year, they had a Greek singer, a young, handsome, dark singer, who was getting up on the tables and was dancing and singing like in "bouzoukea," in Athens. All my memories of Greece were coming alive, and the dancer came to our table. At the end of the song, he leaned down and kissed me passionately on the mouth, while the people in the room were cheering.

That evening, when we went to our cars, my friend asked me to kiss him, the way I just kissed the Greek dancer. And I obliged him. If I was drunk before that, I was not drunk after that. I got scared. After all, his wife was there.

From that moment it was just a question of time. Neither he, nor I, or anybody from outside could stop things. They started to slide rapidly on a steep slope and nobody could have stopped them. Not even his wife. But then, she did not even try. For her, it was her third marriage. She knew better than to intervene. She gave him all the freedom he wanted, with the condition that she kept the money and that he did not divorce her, or that it became a public scandal. She found herself a boyfriend and whished her husband to have a good time. She had all their possessions put in her name, and his salary went directly to her. He was living on an allowance from his wife, while he was working and she was staying home. Hard to believe, but he appreciated the fact that she understood and gave him his freedom and was kind of proud of the way she handled the situation. Very cool! In my opinion, she did not love him. She loved to be his wife, and share his fortune and his social position, but as far as love was concerned, she was the coldest, most calculating woman I ever met.

For me, there was not a chance to win. I sincerely, hopelessly, loved him. I could not live with the compromise. I wanted it all or nothing at all. So, eventually, I was the one to walk out. She kept her husband, for what it was worth.

As he used to say in the beginning, the hardest part to deal with was the sweetness of the love. He was one of those persons with both feet on the ground. He knew the best places to visit, the best places to eat, the best foods, the best hotels and restaurants. I remember, the time we were in New Orleans and started the morning by getting drunk on "hurricanes" and walking back and forth on Bourbon Street in the French Quarters. At about six o'clock in the evening we went to O'Brian's Irish pub and listened to the two piano players and the mixed crowd of people in the audience, singing along with them, and getting more drunk. The next morning we went to the "Café a la Paix" and had latte and *beignets*. I remember the trip back to Jacksonville, and him singing every tune on the radio, stopping at McDonald's and taking burgers and fries and eating them on the car while driving.

I remember, the time we went to Miami and to Miami Beach hotels for drinks and dancing, late in the night.

I remember, going to Ocala, to the Wild Waters Park and riding the water flumes all day like little kids and having a pic-nick in the park.

I remember, going to Bush Gardens in Tampa, and riding the "Scorpion" and me getting so sick to my stomach I thought I would die. On the ride back home, to Jacksonville, I refused to lie back on my seat, but preferred to crowd him for fear of dying alone.

I remember, when we were going fishing in his boat on Roadman Lake, next to the barrage, and went through the army corps locks. I remember speeding with the boat on the springs on our way to the lake.

I remember, the time I took him to Tarpons Springs, the town in the south of Florida, and we eating Greek food, in a small restaurant at night, and those people looking at us. We were so much in love.

But of course, everything was wrong. After our time together, inevitable, he went home, back to his wife, who was nice to him and even nicer to me, sickening nice. Practically, I did not have a chance to win, and I did not see it!

When my family arrived to Jacksonville, they started to bring things to my attention and open my eyes. They were very much against the relationship.

It all ended when I got convinced, without a trace of a doubt, that he was not going to divorce his wife, and that his first loyalty, if not his love, was with his wife.

It took me two years to get over it. It was the hardest thing I ever had to do. One day, I was looking at myself in the bathroom mirror and saw that I was fat, and my eyes were dull, dead, and I decided that I cannot do this to myself any longer; that there has to be life after death, and I wanted to live. Then, I decided to join a fitness center and actively pursue new relationships.

I was through with my morning.

Indeed, there is life after death; one has to have the courage to seek it.

www.ingramcontent.com/pod-product-compliance
Lightning Source LLC
Chambersburg PA
CBHW061036050726
47592CB00004B/1474